The Motorcycle Diaries

T.W. · 11ms from AFW.
Oct. 20th '98

THE MOTORCYCLE DIARIES
A Journey around South America

———◆———

ERNESTO CHE GUEVARA

Translated by

Ann Wright

VERSO
London · New York

First published by Verso 1995
This edition © Verso 1995
Translation © Ann Wright 1995
Paperback edition published by Verso 1996
Reprinted 1996, 1997 (twice)
First published as *Latinoamericana. Un diario per un viaggio in motocicletta*
© Giangiacomo Feltrinelli Editore, Milan 1993
Original title *Notas de viaje*
© Ernesto Che Guevara 1992

Plates (nos 2, 4, 6, 9, 10, 14, 16) © The Hulton Picture Library

The publishers would like to thank Lucia Alvarez de Toledo for her invaluable help and advice during the preparation of this book.

Verso
UK: 6 Meard Street, London W1V 3HR
USA: 180 Varick Street, New York NY 10014-4606

Verso is the imprint of New Left Books

ISBN 1 85984 066 3

British Library Cataloguing in Publication Data
A catalogue record for this book is available from the British Library

Library of Congress Cataloging-in-Publication Data
A catalog record for this book is available from the Library of Congress

Typeset by York House Typographic Ltd, London
Printed and bound in the USA by
R.R. Donnelley & Sons, Harrisonburg, VA

Ernesto Guevara de la Serna's travel diaries, transcribed by Che's Personal Archive in Havana, recount the trials, vicissitudes and tremendous adventure of a young man's journey of discovery through Latin America. Ernesto began writing these diaries when, in December 1951, he set off with his friend Alberto Granado on their long-awaited trip from Buenos Aires, down the Atlantic coast of Argentina, across the Pampa, through the Andes and into Chile, and from Chile northward to Peru and Colombia and finally to Caracas.

These experiences were later rewritten by Ernesto himself as a narrative, offering the reader a deeper insight into Che's life, especially at a little known stage, and revealing details of his personality, his cultural background and his narrative skill — the genesis of a style which he develops in his later works. The reader can also witness the extraordinary change which takes place in him as he discovers Latin America, gets right to its very heart and develops a growing sense of a Latin American identity which makes him a precursor of the new history of America.

Che's Personal Archive,[1]
'Che Guevara' Latin American Centre,
Havana, Cuba

---

[1] Edited by Aleida March de la Torre, Guevara's second wife whom he met and married in Cuba.

A Biographical Chronology

1928   Ernesto Guevara de la Serna is born on 14 June in Rosario, Argentina. The son of Ernesto Guevara Lynch, a construction engineer, and Celia de la Serna, he is the first of five children.

1932   The family moves from Buenos Aires to Alta Gracia, Córdoba, because of the young Ernesto's serious asthma attacks.

The Guevaras are a large, well-off, upper middle-class family with liberal, even radical, ideas. Ernesto Guevara Lynch was anti-clerical, pro-Republican during the Spanish Civil War, pro-Allies during the Second World War, and staunchly anti-Peronist.

1948   Guevara enters the University of Buenos Aires to study medicine. He has a keen interest in literature, travel and sport – especially soccer and rugby, despite his asthma which disqualifies him from military service.

1950   Guevara makes a 4,000 mile trip on a moped alone through Northern Argentina.

1951   Guevara undertakes the journey around South America
–52   narrated in this book. He travels with Alberto Granado, a radical doctor friend a few years his senior who specializes in leprology.

1953   Guevara qualifies as a doctor, completing in three years a course which normally takes six.
       He begins his second trip around Latin America.
       In Bolivia he witnesses the worker mobilization and agrarian reform following the National Revolution of 1952.

1954   In Guatemala Guevara sees the radical government headed by Jacobo Arbenz overthrown by the American-backed Castillo Armas and has to escape to Mexico.
       In Mexico he meets Fidel Castro and joins his group training for their planned invasion of Cuba. He is the only foreigner in the group; included because he is a doctor.
       He marries a Peruvian, Hilda Gadea, with whom he has a daughter, Hildita.

1956   Castro's group lands in Cuba in the yacht *Granma* and begins a three-year guerrilla war against the dictatorship of Fulgencio Batista.

1959   After the victory, Guevara is made Governor of the National Bank in Castro's revolutionary government.
       He marries Aleida March de la Torre, with whom he has four children.

1961 Guevara is made Minister for Industry and, at the meeting of the Organization of American States at Punta del Este, Uruguay, he denounces the Alliance for Progress proposed for Latin America by President Kennedy. For the next four years he travels the world as ambassador for Cuba.

1965 Guevara leaves Cuba to engage directly in the international revolutionary struggle. He travels throughout Africa, eventually fighting in the Congo.

1966 He returns to Latin America to organize a series of guerrilla groups, aiming to spark off 'twenty new Vietnams'. Guevara himself travels in disguise to Bolivia.

1967 Following several months of skirmishes with the Bolivian army, Guevara is captured on 8 October near the town of Vallegrande and executed by order of President Barrientos.

Prologue: Ernesto and Alberto Granado's Journey [2]

BY ERNESTO GUEVARA LYNCH

Alberto Granado, a biochemist and brother of Ernesto's school-friends Tomás and Gregorio, asked Ernesto to join him on a journey through South America. This was in 1951. At the time Ernesto was involved with a charming young girl from Córdoba. My family and I were all convinced he would marry her.

One day Ernesto announced: 'I'm off to Venezuela, Dad.'

Imagine my surprise when I asked, 'How long will you be away?' and he said, 'A year.'

'What about your girlfriend?' I asked.

'If she loves me, she'll wait,' came the reply.

I was used to my son's sudden enthusiasms but I knew he was very keen on her and thought it would dampen his thirst for new horizons. I was puzzled. I didn't understand Ernesto. There were things about him I couldn't quite fathom. They

---

[2] The prologue and epilogue of this edition of *The Motorcycle Diaries* have been taken from Ernesto Guevara Lynch, *Mi hijo el Che* (My Son Che), Editorial Arte y Literatura, Havana, 1988.

only became clear with time. I didn't realize then that his obsession with travelling was just another part of his zeal for learning. He knew that really to understand the needs of the poor he had to travel the world, not as a tourist stopping to take pretty pictures and enjoy the scenery, but in the way he did, by sharing the human suffering found at every bend in the road and looking for the causes of that misery. His journeys were a form of social research, going out to see for himself, but trying at the same time to relieve suffering if he could.

Only with that kind of determination and empathy, a heart devoid of bitterness and a willingness to sacrifice himself for others could he delve into that destitute condition of humanity which sadly is the lot of most of the world's poor. Years later, thinking back over his continuous travelling, I realized that it had convinced him of his true destiny.

After Ernesto left for Venezuela, I was having lunch with one of my sisters and a friend of hers, Father Cuchetti, a priest well known in Argentina for his liberal ideas. I told them about the part of the journey through the Amazon jungle and what Ernesto and Granado had done in the San Pablo leper colony. He listened attentively to my description of the terrible life the lepers led and said: 'My friend, I feel capable of any sacrifice for my fellow man, but I assure you that living with lepers in unhygienic conditions in the tropics, morning, noon and night, is something I could not do. I just couldn't do it. I take my hat off to your son and his friend's humanity and integrity, because to do what they're doing takes more than just guts: you need a will of iron and an enormously compassionate and charitable soul. Your son will go far.'

Truth to tell I was so used to following Ernesto on his travels in my imagination that I hadn't stopped to ponder too deeply what motivated him. In particular, I was fooled by the casual way he talked about his travels, as if it were something easy which anyone could do. He dispensed with any great drama and, maybe so as not to worry our family, pretended to be spurred on by mere curiosity.

Only much later, through his letters, did we come to understand that he was following a true missionary impulse which never left him. His stories, always lively and interesting, had an ironic edge to them so the confused listener never knew whether he was joking or serious.

I remember him writing from Peru one day saying he was heading north. It went something like this: 'If you don't hear from us for a year, look for our shrunken heads in some Yankee museum, because we'll be crossing Jíbaro country and they're expert head hunters.' We knew who the Jíbaros were and we also knew that for centuries they'd shrunk their enemies' heads. That put a different complexion on things: it was no longer a joke; there was a fair dose of truth in it.

I suffered in silence every time Ernesto decided to go off exploring. When he told me of the journey he planned with Granado, I took him aside and said: 'You've some hard times ahead. How can I advise against it when it's something I've always dreamed of myself? But remember, if you get lost in those jungles and I don't hear from you at reasonable intervals, I'll come looking for you, trace your steps, and won't come back till I find you.' He knew I'd do it and I thought it might inhibit his pursuit of danger. I asked him always to leave signs of his whereabouts and send us his itineraries. He did this in his

3

letters. It was also through his letters that we realized the true nature of our son's vocation. They gave us an economic, political and social analysis of all the countries he passed through and also included thoughts which suggested growing leanings towards Communism.

This wasn't a hobby for Ernesto and we knew it. We gradually began to appreciate the magnitude of the undertaking. He had the potential to do whatever he wanted, but potential isn't always enough; actually turning the dreams, plans and hopes into reality is the most difficult part. Ernesto had faith in himself as well as the will to succeed, and a tremendous determination to achieve what he set out to do. Add to this an intelligence of which he gave ample evidence and you can understand how he achieved so much in such a short time.

He was now setting out with Alberto Granado in the footsteps of so many legendary explorers of the Americas. Like them, they would leave behind comfort, emotional ties and families, and go in search of new horizons: Granado, perhaps, bent on discovering new worlds; Ernesto with the same aim, but also the mystical and certain knowledge of his own destiny. So Ernesto and his friend were to follow the path of the *conquistadores*, except that while the latter thirsted for conquest, these two went with quite a different purpose.

Itinerary of the Journey round Latin America

ARGENTINA

- Córdoba, December 1951
- Leave Buenos Aires, 4 January 1952
- Villa Gesell, 6 January
- Miramar, 13 January
- Necochea, 14 January
- Bahía Blanca, arrive 16 January, leave 21 January
- En route for Choele Choel, 22 January
- Choele Choel, 25 January
- Piedra del Aguila, 29 January
- San Martín de los Andes, 31 January
- Nahuel Huapí, 8 February
- Bariloche, 11 February

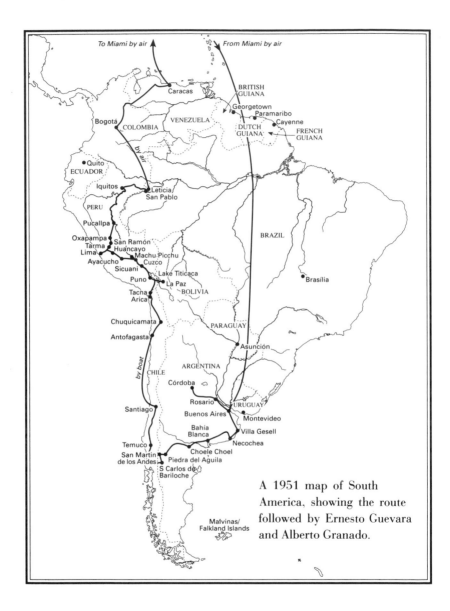

To Miami by air

From Miami by air

Caracas

BRITISH
GUIANA

Georgetown
Paramaribo
Cayenne

Bogotá
COLOMBIA
VENEZUELA
DUTCH
GUIANA
FRENCH
GUIANA

by air

Quito
ECUADOR

Iquitos
Leticia
San Pablo

PERU

Pucallpa

Oxapampa
Tarma
Lima
Ayacucho

San Ramón
Huancayo
Machu Picchu
Cuzco

Sicuani

Puno

Lake Titicaca
La Paz
BOLIVIA

BRAZIL

Brasilia

Tacna
Arica

Chuquicamata

Antofagasta

PARAGUAY

by boat
CHILE

ARGENTINA

Córdoba

Asunción

Santiago

Rosario
Buenos Aires

URUGUAY

Montevideo

Bahía
Blanca

Villa Gesell

Temuco
San Martin
de los Andes
Piedra del Aguila
Choele Choel

Necochea

S Carlos de
Bariloche

Malvinas/
Falkland Islands

A 1951 map of South
America, showing the route
followed by Ernesto Guevara
and Alberto Granado.

6

CHILE

— Peulla, 14 February
— Temuco, 18 February
— Lautaro, 21 February
— Los Angeles, 27 February
— Santiago de Chile, 1 March
— Valparaíso, 7 March
— Aboard the *San Antonio*, 8–10 March
— Antofagasta, 11 March
— Baquedano, 12 March
— Chuquicamata, 13–15 March
— Iquique, 20 March. Toco, La Rica Aventura and Prosperidad Nitrate Companies
— Arica, 22 March

PERU

— Tacna, 24 March
— Tarata, 25 March
— Puno, 26 March
— They sail on Lake Titicaca on 27 March
— Juliaca, 28 March
— Sicuani, 30 March
— Cuzco, 31 March to 3 April
— Machu Picchu, 4–5 April
— Cuzco, 6–7 April
— Abancay, 11 April

- Huancarama, 13 April
- Huambo, 14 April
- Huancarama, 15 April
- Andahuaylas, 16–19 April
- Huanta
- Ayacucho, 22 April
- Huancayo
- La Merced, 25–26 April
- Between Oxapampa and San Ramón, 27 April
- San Ramón, 28 April
- Tarma, 30 April
- Lima, 1–17 May
- Cerro de Pasco, 19 May
- Pucallpa, 24 May
- Aboard *La Cenepa* sailing down the River Ucayali, a tributary of the Amazon, 25–31 May
- Iquitos, 1–5 June
- Aboard *El Cisne* sailing to the leper colony of San Pablo, 6–7 June
- San Pablo, leper colony, 8–20 June
- Aboard the raft *Mambo-Tango* on the Amazon, 21 June

COLOMBIA

- Leticia, 23 June to 1 July. They leave by plane on 2 July
- In transit in Tres Esquinas, 2 July
- Madrid, military airport 30 kilometres from Bogotá
- Bogotá, 2–10 July
- Cúcuta, 12–13 July

VENEZUELA

— San Cristóbal, 14 July
— Between Barquisimeto and Corona, 16 July
— Caracas, 17–26 July

The Motorcycle Diaries

LET'S GET THINGS STRAIGHT

THIS isn't a tale of derring-do, nor is it merely some kind of 'cynical account'; it isn't meant to be, at least. It's a chunk of two lives running parallel for a while, with common aspirations and similar dreams. In nine months a man can think a lot of thoughts, from the height of philosophical conjecture to the most abject longing for a bowl of soup – in perfect harmony with the state of his stomach. And if, at the same time, he's a bit of an adventurer, he could have experiences which might interest other people and his random account would read something like this diary.

So, the coin was tossed, turned somersaults; sometimes coming up heads, sometimes tails. Man, the measure of all things, speaks through my mouth and recounts in my own words what my eyes saw. Out of ten possible heads I may have only seen one tail, or vice versa: there are no excuses; my mouth says what my eyes told it. Was our view too narrow, too biased, too hasty, were our conclusions too rigid? Maybe so, but this is how the typewriter interprets the disparate impulses which made you press the keys, and those fleeting impulses are dead. Besides, no one is answerable to them. The person who wrote these notes died the day he stepped back on Argentine soil. The person who is reorganizing and polishing them, me, is no longer me, at least I'm not the me I was. Wandering around our 'America with a capital A' has changed me more than I thought.

Any book on photographic technique can show you the image of a nocturnal landscape with the full moon shining and the accompanying text revealing the secret of this sunlit darkness. But the reader doesn't really know what kind of sensitive fluid covers my retina, I'm hardly aware of it myself, so you can't examine the plate to find out the actual moment it was taken. If I present a nocturnal picture, you have to take it or leave it, it's not important. Unless you actually know the landscape my diary photographed, you've no option but to accept my version. I now leave you with myself, the man I once was . . .

PRODROMES

I T WAS an October morning. I'd taken advantage of the holiday on the 17th[3] and gone to Córdoba. We were under the vine at Alberto Granado's, drinking sweet maté,[4] com-

[3] At that time this was a national holiday to commemorate Juan Perón's release from prison in 1945. General Perón was President of Argentina from 1946 to 1955 and from 1973 until his death in 1974.
[4] This is the Argentine national drink, a herb tea which is passed round, drunk from a gourd through a long metal utensil with a silver tip.

menting on the latest events in this 'wretched life', and tinkering with La Poderosa II.[5] Alberto was grumbling about having had to quit his job at the leper colony in San Francisco del Chañar and how badly paid he now was at the Hospital Español. I'd also had to quit my job but, unlike him, I was happy to leave. Still, I was restless too, mainly because I was a dreamer and a free spirit; I was fed up with medical school, hospitals and exams.

Our fantasizing took us to faraway places, sailing tropical seas, travelling through Asia. And suddenly, slipping in as if part of our fantasy, came the question: 'Why don't we go to North America?'

'North America? How?'

'On La Poderosa, man.'

That's how the trip came about, and it never deviated from the general principle laid down then: improvisation. Alberto's brothers joined us and a round of maté sealed our pact not to give up until our dream was a reality. Next came the tedious business of chasing visas, certificates and documents, and overcoming all the hurdles modern nations put in the way of would-be travellers. To save face, just in case, we decided to say we were going to Chile. My main task before leaving was to take exams in as many subjects as possible; Alberto's to get the bike ready for the long journey and study the route. At that stage the momentousness of our endeavour hadn't dawned on us, all we could see was the dusty road ahead and us on our bike devouring kilometres in the flight northward.

[5] A Norton 500 motorcycle, literally 'the powerful one'.

DISCOVERING THE OCEAN

THE FULL moon, silhouetted over the sea, showers the waves with silvery sparks. Sitting on a dune, watching the continuous ebb and flow, we each think our different thoughts. For me, the sea has always been a confidant, a friend which absorbs all you tell it without betraying your secrets, and always gives the best advice – a sound you can interpret as you wish. For Alberto, it is a new, oddly perturbing spectacle, reflected in the intensity with which his gaze follows every wave swelling then dying on the beach. At almost thirty, Alberto is seeing the Atlantic for the first time and is over-whelmed by a discovery which opens up infinite routes to all points of the globe. The fresh breeze fills the senses with the power of the sea, it transforms all it touches; even Come-back[6] gazes, his funny little snout aloft, at the silver ribbon unfurling before him several times a minute. Come-back is a symbol and a survivor: a symbol of the bond demanding my return; a survivor of his own mishaps – two crashes in which his little bag flew off the back of the bike, being trodden underfoot by a horse, and persistent diarrhoea.

We're in Villa Gesell, north of Mar del Plata, being enter-tained by an uncle of mine, and taking stock of our first 1,200 kilometres – supposedly the easiest, yet they've already taught us a healthy respect for distances. Whether we make it or not, it's going to be tough, that's obvious already. Alberto laughs at

[6] In English in the original, this is the name of a little dog Ernesto is taking to his girlfriend Chichina, who is on holiday in Miramar, as a symbol of his return.

his minutely detailed plans for the trip, according to which we should already be on the last lap when in fact we're only just starting out.

We left Gesell well stocked with vegetables and tinned meat 'donated' by my uncle. He asked us to send a telegram if we reach Bariloche so he can buy a lottery ticket with the same number as the telegram; a bit of an exaggeration, we thought. Others added, 'The bike's a good excuse for jogging,' and so on. We're determined to prove them wrong, but a natural apprehension keeps us from advertising our mutual confidence.

Along the coast road Come-back keeps up his affinity for aviation but emerges unscathed from a fresh head-on bang. The bike is very hard to control because the extra weight on a rack behind the centre of gravity lifts the front wheel at the slightest lapse in concentration and sends us flying. We stop at a butcher's and buy some meat to grill and milk for the dog, who won't touch it. I begin to worry more about the animal's health than the cash I'd coughed up for it. The meat turns out to be horse. It's incredibly sweet and we can't eat it. Fed up, I chuck a bit away and the dog wolfs it down in no time. Amazed, I throw it another piece and the same thing happens. The milk regime is lifted. In Miramar, in the midst of the uproar caused by Come-back's admirers, I enter a ...

... ROMANTIC INTERLUDE

I T ISN'T really the purpose of this diary to recount the days in Miramar where Come-back found a new home, at one of whose residents in particular the name was directed. The trip hung in the balance, in a cocoon, subordinate to the word which consents and ties.

Alberto saw the danger and was already imagining himself alone on the highways and byways of America, but he said nothing. The tug of war was between her and me. For a moment Otero Silva's poem[7] rang in my ears as I left, I thought, victorious:

> I heard on the boat
> Wet feet splashing
> And felt faces dusk with hunger
> My heart a pendulum between her and the street
> What strength broke me free from her eyes
> Loose from her arms
> She stood tears clouding her grief
> Behind rain and window pane
> But unable to cry: Wait
> I'll go with you!

Afterwards I wasn't sure if driftwood had the right to say 'I succeeded' when the tide threw it up on the beach it sought; but that was later. Later is of no interest to now. The two days I'd planned stretched like elastic into eight and with the bitter-

---

[7] Miguel Otero Silva, left-wing Venezuelan poet and novelist, was born in 1908. The free version of the poem is by the translator.

sweet taste of the goodbye mingling with my inveterate halitosis I finally felt myself wafted away on the winds of adventure towards worlds which I fancied stranger than they were, in situations I imagined much more normal than they turned out to be.

I remember the day my friend the sea decided to come to my aid and rescue me from limbo. The beach was deserted and a cold wind blew towards the land. My head lay in the lap which tied me to these shores. The whole universe floated rhythmically by, obeying impulses from my voice within, lulled by everything around. Suddenly a stronger gust of wind brought a different voice from the sea; I lifted my head in surprise, it was nothing, a false alarm. I settled my head back, returned my dreams to the caressing lap again, when I heard the sea's warning once more. Its vast discordant rhythm hammered at the fortress in me and threatened its imposing serenity. We felt cold and left the beach, fleeing the perturbing presence which refused to leave me. On that small stretch of beach the sea pranced about indifferent to its eternal law and spawned the note of caution, the warning. But a man in love (Alberto used a juicier, less literary word) is in no condition to listen to that kind of signal; in the great belly of the Buick the bourgeois side of my universe was still under construction.

The first commandment for every good explorer is: An expedition has two points; the point of departure and the point of arrival. If you want to make the second theoretical point coincide with the actual point, don't think about the means (the expedition is a hypothetical space which ends where it ends, so there are as many means as there are means to an end, that is, the means are limitless).

I remembered Alberto's exhortation: 'The bracelet or you're not who you think you are.'

Her hands disappeared in the hollow of mine.

'Chichina, that bracelet . . . Can I take it to guide me and remind me of you?'

Poor thing! I know the gold didn't matter, despite what they say: her fingers were merely weighing up the love that made me ask for it. At least, that's what I honestly think. Alberto says (a bit mischievously, I feel), that you don't need very sensitive fingers to weigh up the twenty-nine carats of my love.

CUTTING THE LAST TIES

O UR NEXT stop was Necochea where an old university friend of Alberto's had his practice. We made it easily in a morning, arriving just at steak time, and received a cordial welcome from the friend and a not so cordial one from his wife who saw danger in our resolutely bohemian ways.

'You qualify as a doctor in a year's time yet you're going away? And you've no idea when you'll be back. Why?'

Not getting a precise answer to her desperate whys and wherefores made her hair stand on end. She treated us courteously but her hostility was plain despite the fact she knew (I think she knew) victory was hers, that her husband was beyond 'redemption'.

In Mar del Plata we'd visited a doctor friend of Alberto's who had joined the Party,[8] with all the privileges that entailed. This

---

[8] The Peronist Party.

one in Necochea remained faithful to his – the Radicals – yet we were as remote from one as from the other. Radicalism, which had never been a tenable political position for me, was also losing its grip on Alberto who had been friendly at one time with certain of the leaders he respected. When we mounted our bike again, after thanking the couple for giving us three days of the good life, we journeyed on to Bahía Blanca, feeling a little lonelier but a good deal freer. Friends were expecting us there too, friends of mine this time, and they also offered us generous and cordial hospitality. We spent several days in this southern port, fixing the bike and wandering round the city. These were the last days when we did not have to think about money. A rigid diet of meat, polenta and bread would have to be followed to the letter to stretch our pathetic monetary resources. Bread now tasted of warning: 'I won't be so easy to get soon, man.' And we swallowed it with all the more gusto. Like camels, we wanted to store up reserves for what lay ahead.

The night before our departure, I came down with quite a high temperature, which made us a day late leaving Bahía Blanca. We finally left at three in the afternoon, under a blazing sun which was even hotter by the time we reached the sand dunes round Médanos. The bike, with its badly distributed load, kept leaping out of control and spinning over. Alberto fought a stubborn duel with the sand which he insists he won. The truth is that we found ourselves resting comfortably on our backsides in the sand six times before we finally got out on to the flat. We did get out, however, and this is my comrade's main argument for claiming victory over Médanos.

Setting off again, I took the controls and accelerated to make up for lost time. A fine sand covered part of the bend and, wham: the worst crash of our whole expedition. Alberto came out unscathed but the cylinder trapped my foot and scorched it, leaving an unpleasant souvenir for a long time because the wound didn't heal.

A heavy downpour forced us to seek shelter at an *estancia*,[9] but to reach it we had to go three hundred metres up a muddy track which sent us flying another couple of times. The welcome was magnificent but the toll of our first experience on unpaved roads was alarming: nine spills in a single day. However, lying on camp beds, the only beds we'd know from now on, beside La Poderosa, our snail-like abode, we looked into the future with impatient joy. We seemed to breathe more freely, a lighter air, an air of adventure. Faraway countries, heroic deeds, beautiful women whirled round and round in our turbulent imaginations. But in tired eyes which nevertheless refused sleep, a pair of green dots representing the world I'd left mocked the freedom I sought, hitching their image to my fantasy flight across the lands and seas of the world.

REMEDY FOR FLU: BED

THE BIKE snorted with boredom along the long accident-free road and we snorted with fatigue. Driving on a gravel-covered road had changed a pleasant spree into a heavy

---

[9] A farm or cattle ranch in Argentina.

chore. And a whole day of taking turns at the controls had by night-time left us with a greater desire to sleep than to make the effort to reach Choele Choel, a biggish town where there was the chance of free lodging. We stopped in Benjamín Zorrilla and settled down comfortably in a room at the railway station. We slept like logs.

The next morning we got up early, but when I went to fetch water for our maté, a strange sensation ran through my body followed by a shiver. Ten minutes later I was trembling uncontrollably like a man possessed. My quinine tablets were no use, my head was like a drum beating out strange rhythms, weird colours passed shapelessly round the walls and some desperate retching produced a green vomit. I spent the whole day in that state, unable to eat a thing, until the evening, when I felt fit enough to climb on the bike and, dozing on Alberto's shoulder, reached Choele Choel. We went straight to see Dr Barrera, the director of the little hospital and a member of parliament. He received us amiably, giving us a room to sleep in. He put me on a course of penicillin which lowered my temperature within four hours, but whenever we talked about leaving the doctor shook his head and said, 'For flu: bed.' (That was the diagnosis, for want of a better one.) So we spent several days there, being looked after like royalty. Alberto took a photo of me in my hospital garb. I looked awful: gaunt, huge eyes, a beard whose ridiculous shape didn't change much in the following months. It's a shame it wasn't a good photo; it documented our changed circumstances, our new horizons, free from the shackles of 'civilization'.

One morning the doctor didn't shake his head in the usual fashion and that was enough. We were gone within the hour, heading west towards the lakes, our next destination. Our bike struggled, showing signs it was feeling the strain, especially in the bodywork which we constantly had to fix with Alberto's favourite spare part – wire. I don't know where he picked up this quote, which he attributed to Oscar Gálvez:[10] 'Where a piece of wire can replace a screw, give me the wire, it's safer.' Our trousers and hands were proof that we sided with Gálvez, at least as far as wire was concerned.

Night had fallen and we were trying to reach human habitation: we had no lights and spending the night in the open is not pleasant. We were going along slowly with a torch when there was a strange noise we couldn't identify. The torch didn't give enough light to find the cause of the noise so we had to camp right there. We settled down for the night as best we could, put up our tent and crawled into it, hoping to smother our hunger and thirst (there was no water near by and we had no meat) with some exhausted sleep. However, in no time the evening breeze had turned into a violent gale which uprooted our tent and exposed us to the elements, to the worsening cold. We had to tie the bike to a telegraph pole and, putting the tent over it for protection, lie down behind it. The semi-hurricane prevented us from using our camp beds. It wasn't a pleasant night at all, but sleep finally triumphed over the cold, wind and everything else, and we woke at nine in the morning with the sun high over our heads.

In the light of day, we discovered that the famous noise had been the front part of the bike frame breaking. We now had to fix it as best we could and find a town where we could weld the

[10] An Argentine champion rally driver.

broken bar. Our friend, the wire, solved our problem provisionally. We packed up and set off not knowing exactly how far we were from the nearest habitation. Imagine our surprise when, coming out of the next bend, we saw a house. They received us very well and appeased our hunger with exquisite roast lamb. From there we walked twenty kilometres to a place called Piedra del Águila where we could weld the part, but it was so late by then that we decided to spend the night in the mechanic's house.

Except for a couple more minor spills which didn't damage the bike too much, we continued calmly on towards San Martín de los Andes. We were almost there, and I was driving, when we took our first tumble in the South on a beautiful gravel bend by a babbling brook. This time La Poderosa's bodywork was damaged enough to make us stop and, to cap it all, we had what we most dreaded: a punctured back tyre. To be able to mend it, we had to take off all the luggage, undo all the wire securing the rack, then struggle with the wheel cover which defied our pathetic crowbar. This flat tyre (lazily done, I admit) lost us two hours. Late in the afternoon we stopped at an *estancia* whose owners, very welcoming Germans, had in the past put up an uncle of mine, an inveterate old traveller whose example I was now emulating. They said we could fish in the river flowing through the *estancia*. Alberto cast his line, and before he knew what was happening, he had a fleeting form glinting in the sunlight jumping about on the end of his hook. It was a rainbow trout, a beautiful fish, succulent and fleshy (at least it was when baked and seasoned by our hunger). I prepared the fish while Alberto cast his line again and again, but he didn't get a single bite despite hours of trying. It was dark by then, so we had to spend the night in the farm labourers' kitchen.

At five in the morning, the huge stove which occupies the middle of this kind of kitchen was lit and the whole place filled with smoke. The farm labourers passed round their bitter maté and cast aspersions on our own 'girlish' maté, as they call sweet maté in those parts. They weren't very communicative on the whole, typical of the subjugated Araucanian race, still wary of the white man who in the past brought them so much misfortune and still exploits them. When we asked about the land and their work, they answered by shrugging their shoulders and saying 'don't know' or 'maybe', which ended the conversation.

We also had the chance to gorge ourselves on cherries, so much so that when we went on to the plums I'd had enough and went to lie down to digest it all. Alberto had some so as not to seem rude. Up the trees we ate like pigs, as if we were in a race to the finish. One of the owner's sons seemed to think these disgustingly dressed and apparently famished 'doctors' a bit odd, but he said nothing and let us eat to our heart's content, to the point where we had to walk slowly to avoid kicking our own stomachs.

We mended the kick-start and other minor defects and set off again for San Martín de los Andes where we arrived just before dark.

SAN MARTÍN DE LOS ANDES

THE ROAD winds between the rolling foothills of the great cordillera of the Andes, then descends steeply as it reaches a town which is ugly and sad in itself but surrounded by magnificent, densely wooded mountains. San Martín lies on the yellow-green slopes which sink into the blue depths of Lake Lacar, a tongue of water five hundred metres wide and thirty-five kilometres long. The town's climate and transport problems were solved the day it was 'discovered' as a tourist spot and its bread and butter secured.

Our first assault on the local clinic failed miserably but we were told to try the same tactic at the National Parks offices. The park superintendent gave us permission to stay in one of the toolsheds. The nightwatchman arrived, a great fat man weighing 140 kilos with a face as hard as nails, but he was very nice to us, letting us cook in his hut. That first night was great; we slept on straw in the shed, snug and warm. You certainly need it in those parts where the nights are cold.

We bought some beef and set off to walk along the lakeside. There, in the shade of the huge trees, where the wilderness had held back the advance of civilization, we made plans to set up a laboratory when we got back from our trip. We imagined enormous windows looking out over the lake, while winter painted the ground white; an autogiro to get from one side to the other; fishing from a boat; endless excursions into the almost virgin forest.

Often on our travels, we longed to stay in some of the wonderful places we saw, but only the Amazon jungle had the same strong pull on the sedentary part of ourselves as this did.

I now know, by a fatalistic coincidence with fact, that I am destined to travel, or rather, *we* are destined, because Alberto is just like me. All the same, there are moments when I think with profound longing of those wonderful areas in the South of Argentina. Maybe one day when I'm tired of wandering, I'll come back to Argentina and settle in the Andean lakes, if not indefinitely at least in transit to another conception of the world.

We started back at dusk and it was dark before we arrived. We were pleasantly surprised to find that Don Pedro Olate, the nightwatchman, was treating us to a barbecue. We contributed wine to return the gesture and ate like lions, for a change. Talking about how good the meat was and how we soon wouldn't be eating it as extravagantly as we did in Argentina, Don Pedro said he'd been asked to organize a barbecue for the drivers of a motor race taking place that coming Sunday on the local track. He'd need two helpers and offered us the job. 'You may not get paid, but you can stock up on meat.'

It seemed a good idea and we accepted the jobs of assistants Number One and Two to the 'The Barbecue King of Southern Argentina'.

Sunday was awaited with almost religious dedication by us two assistants. At six in the morning we started loading wood on to a lorry bound for the barbecue site and kept working until eleven when the signal was given and everyone threw themselves voraciously on to the tasty ribs.

Giving orders was a very odd person whom I addressed with the utmost respect as 'Señora' every time I spoke, until one of my fellow workers said: 'Hey, kid, don't push Don Pendón too far, he'll get angry.'

'Who's Don Pendón?' I said, with what's considered a rude gesture of the hand. The answer, that Don Pendón was the 'Señora', stopped me in my tracks, but not for long.

As usual at barbecues, there was much too much meat for the number of guests, so we had carte blanche to follow our vocation as camels. We also put into action a carefully conceived plan. I pretended to get drunker and drunker and, with every attack of nausea, would stagger off to the stream, with a bottle of red wine under my leather jacket. I had five of these attacks, and the same number of litres of red were stored under a willow branch, keeping cool in the water. When the whole thing was over and the time came to pack up the lorry and go back to town, I, true to my role, worked very grudgingly, quarrelled with Don Pendón and finally lay flat on my back on the grass unable to take another step. Alberto, good friend that he is, apologized for me to the boss and stayed behind to look after me as the lorry left. When the noise of the engine faded in the distance, we sprinted off like young colts to get the wine which would guarantee us a few days of oligarchically irrigated food. Alberto got there first and threw himself under the willow. His face was a picture. There wasn't a single bottle there. Someone had not been fooled by my drunken state, or had seen me sneak off with the wine. The fact was we were back at square one, going over in our minds the smiles which had greeted my drunken antics, trying to find some trace of irony which would identify the thief, but all to no avail. Carrying the bit of bread and cheese we'd been given and a few kilos of meat for the night, we had to walk back to town, well wined and dined, but well depressed too; not so much because of the wine, but because of the fools they'd made of us. Can you imagine!

The next day was rainy and cold. We thought the race would be abandoned and were waiting for the rain to ease off so we could go and cook some meat by the lake when we heard over the loudspeakers that the race was still on. In our role as barbecue assistants we got in free and, comfortably installed, watched a pretty good race of Argentine drivers.

We were thinking of moving on and discussing the merits of different routes, drinking maté in the doorway of our shed, when a jeep pulled up and some friends of Alberto's from distant, almost mythical Villa Concepción del Tío got out. There were lots of friendly hugs all round and we immediately went off to celebrate by filling our bellies with frothy liquids, as is customary on such occasions.

They invited us to visit them in the town where they were working, Junín de los Andes, and we set off, lightening the load on our bike by leaving our gear in the National Parks' shed.

CIRCULAR EXPEDITION

J UNÍN de los Andes, less fortunate than its lakeside brother, vegetates in a backwater of civilization. The attempt to reactivate the town and shake off the monotony of its sleepy existence by building the barracks on which our friends were working has failed dismally. I say our friends, because in no time at all they were mine too.

The first night was spent reminiscing about the distant past in Villa Concepción, enhanced by unlimited supplies of red wine. I had to abandon the match, due to lack of training, but I slept like a log in honour of the proper bed.

The next day was spent fixing a few problems on the bike in our friends' company's workshop. And that night they gave us a magnificent send-off from Argentina: a beef and lamb barbecue, with a delicious salad and scrumptious crackers. So after several days of partying, we were seen off with many hugs on the road to Carrué, another lake in the region. The road is very bad and our poor bike snorted as I tried to push it out of the sand. The first five kilometres took us an hour and a half, but after that the road improved and we arrived without mishap at Carrué Chico, a little green lake surrounded by wild, wooded hills, and then at Carrué Grande, a much bigger lake but impossible to drive round on a bike because there is only the bridle path which local smugglers use to cross over to Chile.

We left the bike at the cabin of a forest warden who wasn't at home and set off to climb the peak facing the lake. It was nearly lunch time and our provisions consisted of a piece of cheese and some preserves. A duck flew over the lake. Alberto quickly calculated the absence of the warden, the distance of the bird, the possibility of a fine, etc., and fired. By a wonderful stroke of good luck (not for it, of course), the duck fell into the lake. A discussion immediately ensued as to who would fetch it. I lost and plunged in. I felt as if icy fingers were clutching my body, so that I could barely move. Allergic as I am to the cold, swimming the twenty metres there and twenty metres back to get Alberto's duck made me suffer like a bedouin. Just as well that roast duck, seasoned as usual by our hunger, is an exquisite dish.

Invigorated by our lunch, we set off enthusiastically on the climb. Setting off with us, however, were gadflies which circled round biting when they got the chance. The climb was difficult because we lacked equipment and experience, but some weary hours later we reached the summit. To our disappointment, there was no panoramic view: neighbouring mountains blocked it; whichever way we looked there was a higher peak in the way.

After a few minutes fooling about in the snow which crowned the peak, we began the task of going down, spurred on by the fact that it would soon be dark.

The first part was easy, but then the stream we were following grew into a torrent with smooth sides and slippery boulders, difficult to walk on. We had to climb through the osiers at the edge and finally reached an area of reeds, thick and treacherous. It was night by now and with it came thousands of uncanny noises and a strange empty sensation with each step we took in the dark. Alberto lost his goggles and my tracksuit bottoms were ripped to shreds. We finally reached the treeline and every step had to be taken with the utmost care because in the pitch black our sixth sense was so heightened we saw abysses every other second.

After an eternity of tramping through muddy ground we recognized the stream which flowed out into the Carrué, the trees disappeared and we reached the flat. The huge figure of a stag dashed across the stream and his body, silvery in the light of the rising moon, disappeared into the undergrowth. This glimpse of nature made our hearts quicken. We walked slowly so as not to disturb the peace of the wild sanctuary with which we were now communing.

We waded across the ribbon of water which left our ankles

tingling from those icy fingers I so loathe and reached the shelter of the warden's cabin. He was kind enough to offer us hot maté and sheepskins to bed down on till morning. It was 12.35 a.m.

We took it slowly on the way back, passing lakes of a hybrid beauty compared to Carrué, and finally reached San Martín where Don Pendón got us ten *pesos* each for the barbecue work, before we set off further south.

EN ROUTE FOR BARILOCHE: LETTER FROM ERNESTO TO HIS MOTHER, JANUARY 1952

DEAR MUM,
I know you've had no news from me, but likewise, I've had none from you and I'm worried. To tell you everything that has happened to us would defeat the purpose of these few lines; I'll just say that shortly after leaving Bahía Blanca, two days later, in fact, I got a temperature of 40 degrees which laid me up for a day. I managed to get up the following day and ended up in the Choele Choel regional hospital where I recovered in four days after a dose of a little known drug: penicillin.

After that, plagued by a thousand problems which we solved with our usual resourcefulness, we reached San Martín de los Andes, a wonderful spot amid virgin forest, with a beautiful lake. You have to see it, it's certainly worthwhile. Our faces are acquiring the texture of carborundum. We've been asking for food, lodging and whatever's going at any house with a garden we see along the road. We happened to end up at the Von Putnamers' *estancia*, friends of Jorge's, especially the Peronist one who's always drunk and the best of the three. I diagnosed a tumour in the occipital zone probably of hydatic origin. We'll see what happens. In two or three days we leave for Bariloche travelling at a leisurely pace. If your letter can get there by 10/12 February, write to me at the poste restante. Well, Mum, the next page is for Chichina. Lots of love to everyone and let me know if Dad is in the South or not. An affectionate hug from your loving son.

THE SEVEN LAKES ROUTE

W E DECIDED to go to Bariloche via the Seven Lakes route, so called because that's how many lakes the road skirts before reaching the town. La Poderosa did the initial kilometres with only a few minor mechanical hitches until, with the night upon us, we did the old broken headlamp trick so we could sleep in a navvy's hut, a handy ruse because it was unusually cold that night. So biting was the cold that a stranger soon appeared asking to borrow a blanket because he and his wife were camping at the lakeside and were freezing. We went to share some maté with this stoical pair who had been living in the Lakes for some time with just a tent and the contents of their rucksacks. They made us feel pathetic.

We set off again along lakes of different sizes surrounded by ancient forests, the scents of nature caressing our nostrils. But strangely enough the sight of a lake, wood, lone house with

neat garden soon begins to pall. Looking at the scenery superficially only captures its boring uniformity and doesn't get into
the spirit of the countryside; for that you need to spend several
days in a place.

We finally reached the northern end of Lake Nahuel Huapí
and slept on the shore, happy and stuffed after a huge barbecue. But when we took to the road again, we noticed a
puncture in the rear wheel and a tedious battle with the inner
tube began. Each time we put a patch on one side, we punctured the other side of the tube, until we had run out of patches
and had to spend the night right there. An Austrian who
worked as a caretaker and who had raced motorbikes in his
youth let us stay in an empty shed, torn between his desire to
help fellow bikers in need and fear of his boss.

In his broken Spanish he told us there was a puma in the
vicinity. 'Pumas are vicious. They're not afraid to attack
people and they have a huge blond mane.'

When we went to close the door we found that only the
bottom half shut; it was like a stable door. I put our revolver by
my head in case the mountain lion, who filled our thoughts,
decided to make an untimely midnight visit. It was just getting
light when I woke to the sound of claws scratching at the door.
Beside me, Alberto was all apprehensive silence. My hand was
tense on the cocked revolver. Two luminous eyes stared at me
from the shadow of the trees. They sprang forward like a
pouncing cat, while the black mass of the body slid over the
door. It was instinctive; the brakes of intelligence failed and
my instinct for preservation pulled the trigger. The thunder
resounded round the walls for a moment and stopped on a
lighted torch in the doorway, shouting at us in desperation.

Our timid silence knew the reason or at least guessed from the caretaker's stentorian tones and the hysterical sobs of his wife bending over the corpse of Bobby, her nasty grumpy dog.

Alberto went to Angostura to get the tyre fixed and I thought I'd have to spend the night in the open because I couldn't ask for a bed in a house where we were considered murderers. Luckily our bike was near another navvy's house and he put me up in the kitchen with a friend of his. At midnight I heard the sound of rain and was going to get up to cover the bike with a tarpaulin. Irritated by the sheepskin which served as a pillow, I decided to take a few puffs from my asthma inhaler. As I did so, my sleeping companion woke up. When he heard the puff, he made a sudden jerky movement, then stayed silent. I sensed his body rigid under his blankets, clutching a knife, holding his breath. With the experience of the previous night, I decided to keep still for fear of being knifed, in case mirages were contagious in those parts.

We reached San Carlos de Bariloche in the evening of the next day and spent the night in the police station waiting for the *Modesta Victoria* to sail over towards the border with Chile.

'I FEEL MY ROOTS SURFACE FREE AND NAKED ... AND ... '

WE WERE in the kitchen of the police station sheltering from the storm unleashing its fury outside. I read and re-read the incredible letter. Suddenly all my dreams of home, bound up with the eyes which saw me off in Miramar, were shattered, apparently for no good reason. An enormous weariness came over me and, half dozing, I listened to the lively chatter of a globetrotting prisoner concocting a thousand exotic brews, safe in his audience's ignorance. I could hear the warm seductive words while the faces around him leaned forward, the better to hear his tales unfold. I could see as if through a distant fog an American doctor we had met there in Bariloche nodding: 'You'll get where you're heading, you've got guts. But I think you'll stay in Mexico. It's a wonderful country.'

I suddenly caught myself flying off with the sailor to distant lands, well away from what my own current drama should be. A feeling of profound unease came over me; that drama didn't affect me. I began to worry about myself and started a weepy letter, but I couldn't, it was hopeless to try.

In the half light, magical figures hovered but 'she' wouldn't appear. I thought I loved her until this moment when I realized I couldn't feel, I had to think her back again. I had to fight for her, she was mine, mine, m . . . I fell asleep.

A warm sun lit the new day, the day we were leaving, our last day on Argentine soil. Getting the bike on to the *Modesta Victoria* wasn't easy, but eventually we did it. And getting it off again wasn't easy either. All the same, there we were in that tiny place by the lake, with the pompous name of Puerto Blest. A few kilometres, three or four at most, and back on water, a dirty green lake this time, Laguna Frías. Another short voyage before reaching customs at last, then the Chilean immigration post on the other side of the cordillera which is much lower at this latitude. There the route crosses yet another lake, fed by the River Tronador which rises in the majestic volcano of the same name. In contrast to the Argentine lakes, the water in this one, Lake Esmeralda, is warm and makes the task of bathing enjoyable; much more to our taste, I may say. Up in the mountains, at a place called Casa Pangue, is a vantage point from where you get a panoramic view over Chile. It's a sort of crossroads, at least it was for me at that particular moment. I was looking to the future, up the narrow strip of Chile and what lay beyond, muttering the lines of the Otero Silva poem.

OBJECTS OF CURIOSITY

THE OLD tub carrying our bike oozed water from every pore. My imagination soared as I bent rhythmically over the pump. A doctor, travelling back from Peulla in the passenger launch serving Lake Esmeralda, passed the contraption our bike was lashed to and where we were paying for both our and La Poderosa's ticket with the sweat of our brows. His face was a picture as he watched us struggling to keep the vessel afloat, almost naked and covered in oily bilge-water.

We'd met several doctors travelling down there to whom we'd held forth on the subject of leprology, embellishing a little here and there. Our colleagues from the other side of the Andes were impressed because, since they don't have that problem in Chile, they didn't have a clue about leprosy and lepers and admitted they'd never ever seen one. They told us about the leper colony on Easter Island which had a small number of lepers; it was a wonderful island, they said, and our scientific appetites were whetted. This one doctor generously offered us any help we might need in view of our 'very interesting journey'. But in those blissful days in the South of Chile, before our bellies were empty and we got really brazen, we just asked him for an introduction to the President of the Friends of Easter Island, who lived near them in Valparaíso. Naturally, they were delighted.

The lake route ended in Petrohué where we said goodbye to everybody; but not before posing for some sweet black Brazilian girls who stuck us in their South of Chile souvenir album and a couple of naturalists from some country or other in Europe who ceremoniously took our addresses so they could send us copies of the photos.

Some character in town wanted a station wagon driven to Osorno which was where we were heading and asked me to do it. With Alberto giving me a quick lesson in gear changes, I went solemnly off to take up my post. Just like in a cartoon, I literally set off with bumps and jerks behind Alberto on the bike. Each bend was a torment: brake, clutch, first, second, help, Mu-um ... The road wound through beautiful countryside along Lake Osorno, with the volcano of the same name standing guard above it, but I was in no state on this accident-studded road to eulogize the scenery. The only accident, however, happened to a little pig who ran in front of the car on a slope before I got the hang of this brake and clutch business.

After we reached Osorno, freeloaded in Osorno, left Osorno, we kept heading north through the delightful Chilean countryside, divided into plots, every bit farmed, in contrast to our own arid south. The Chileans, exceedingly friendly people, welcomed us wherever we went. We finally arrived in the port of Valdivia, on a Sunday. As we strolled round the city, we dropped into the local newspaper, the *Correo de Valdivia*, which wrote a very kind article about us. Valdivia was celebrating its fourth centenary and we dedicated our journey to the city as a tribute to the great explorer whose name it bears. They persuaded us to write a letter to Molinas Luco, the Mayor of Valparaíso, preparing him for our great Easter Island ruse.

The harbour, crammed full of goods we'd never seen before, the market where they sold different foods, the typically Chilean wooden houses, the clothes of the *guasos*,[11] all felt totally different from what we knew back home; there was something indigenously American, untouched by the exoticism which invaded our pampas. This may be because Anglo-Saxon immigrants in Chile don't mix and so preserve the purity of the indigenous race which is practically non-existent in Argentina today.

But with all the differences of customs and language which distinguish Argentina from our thin brother on the other side of the Andes, one particular shout seems international: the 'give them water' which greeted the sight of my calf-length trousers, not some fashion of mine but inherited from a generous but short friend.

THE EXPERTS

C HILEAN hospitality, as I never get tired of saying, is one of the things which make travelling in our neighbouring country so enjoyable. And we enjoyed it to the full, as only we

[11] Chilean peasants.

know how. I awoke lazily under the bedclothes, weighing up the value of a good bed and calculating the calorie content of the previous night's meal. I went over recent events in my mind: La Poderosa's treacherous puncture which left us stranded on the road in the rain; the generous help of Raúl, owner of the bed in which we were now sleeping; and the interview we gave to *El Austral* in Temuco. Raúl was a veterinary student, not a very serious one it seemed, and owned a truck into which he had hoisted our poor old bike and brought us to this quiet town in the middle of Chile. Truth to tell, our friend might at some moment have wished he'd never met us, since we gave him a bad night's sleep, but he'd dug his own grave by bragging about the money he spent on women and inviting us for a night out at a 'cabaret'; all at his expense, naturally. This led to an animated discussion which went on for hours and was why we prolonged our stay in the land of Pablo Neruda. In the end, of course, came the inevitable problem which meant we had to postpone the visit to that very interesting place of entertainment, but to compensate we got bed and board. At one in the morning, there we were cool as you please devouring everything on the table, which was quite a lot, and some more that arrived later. Then we appropriated our host's bed since his father was being transferred to Santiago and there was not much furniture left in the house.

Alberto, dead to the world, was defying the morning sun to penetrate his slumber, while I began dressing slowly, a task which wasn't very difficult because the difference between our night wear and day wear consisted, generally, of shoes. The newspaper had a generous number of pages, unlike our own poor stunted dailies, but I was only interested in one piece of local news which I found in large type in section two: TWO ARGENTINE LEPROLOGY EXPERTS TOUR SOUTH AMERICA BY MOTOR-BIKE. And then in smaller type: 'They are in Temuco and want to visit Rapa-Nui.'

This was our audacity in a nutshell. We, the experts, key figures in the field of leprology in the Americas, with vast experience, having treated three thousand patients, familiar with all the important centres on the continent and their sanitary conditions, had deigned to visit this picturesque, melancholy little town. We assumed they would fully appreciate our respect for the town, but we didn't really know. Soon the whole family had gathered round the article and all the other items in the paper were treated with Olympian contempt. And so, basking in their admiration, we said goodbye to these people of whom we remember nothing, not even their name.

We had asked permission to leave the bike in the garage of a man who lived on the outskirts and we now made our way there, no longer just a pair of reasonably likeable bums with a bike in tow. No, we were now *the experts*, and that's how we were treated. We spent the day fixing the bike and a little dark maid kept coming up with edible treats. At five o'clock, after a sumptuous 'snack' laid on by our host, we said goodbye to Temuco and headed north.

DIFFICULTIES INCREASE

OUR DEPARTURE from Temuco went without a hitch until we were outside town when we noticed the back tyre had a puncture and we had to stop and fix it. We worked hard but no sooner had we put the spare on than we saw it was going down; it had a puncture too. It looked as though we'd have to spend the night in the open as there was no question of mending it at that time of night. However, we weren't just anybody now, we were the experts; we soon found a railway worker who took us to his house where we were treated like kings.

Early next morning we took the inner tubes and tyre to the garage to get some bits of metal removed and the tyre patched again. It was nearly sunset when we finally left, but first we were invited to a typical Chilean meal: tripe and another similar dish, all very spicy, washed down with a delicious rough wine. As usual, Chilean hospitality left us legless.[12]

Naturally we didn't get very far, and less than eighty kilometres on we stopped for the night at a forest warden's who expected a tip. Since it didn't materialize he didn't give us breakfast next morning, so we set off in a bad mood intending to light a fire and make some maté as soon as we'd done a few kilometres. We'd gone a little way and I was looking out for a place to stop when, without warning, the bike suddenly veered sideways and threw us off. Alberto and I, unhurt, examined the bike and found one of the steering columns broken and, even more serious, the gearbox was smashed. It was impossible to go on. All we could do was wait patiently for an obliging lorry to take us to the next town.

A car going the other way stopped and its occupants got out to see what had happened and offer their services. They said whatever two such eminent scientists needed, they would be

---

[12] The phrase in Spanish is: 'left us halfway between San Juan and Mendoza', which are Argentina's largest wine-producing provinces.

only too pleased to help. 'I recognized you straight away from the photo in the paper,' said one. But there was nothing we wanted, except a lorry going the other way. We thanked them and had settled down for our habitual maté when the owner of a nearby shack rushed over and invited us in, and we downed a couple of litres in his kitchen. We were introduced to his *charango*, a musical instrument made with three or four wires about two metres long stretched tightly over two empty tins fixed to a board. The musician has a kind of metal knuckle-duster with which he plucks the strings producing a sound like a toy guitar. Around twelve a van came along and, after much pleading, the driver agreed to take us to the next town, Lautaro. We managed to get space in the best garage in the area and someone to do the soldering, a friendly little guy called Luna who took us home for lunch a couple of times. We divided our time between working on the bike and cadging something to eat in the homes of the many curiosity seekers who came to see us at the garage. Right next door was a German family, or one of German origin, who treated us handsomely. We slept in the local barracks.

The bike was more or less mended and we were all set to leave the following day, so we decided to let our hair down with some of our new pals who invited us for a few drinks. Chilean wine is very good and I was downing it at an amazing rate, so by the time we went on to the village dance I felt ready for anything. It was a very cosy evening and we kept filling our bellies and minds with wine. One of the mechanics from the garage, a particularly nice guy, asked me to dance with his wife because he'd been mixing his drinks and was the worse for wear. His wife was pretty randy and obviously in the mood, and I, full of Chilean wine, took her by the hand to lead her outside. She followed me docilely but then realized her husband was watching and changed her mind. I was in no state to listen to reason and we had a bit of a barney in the middle of the dance floor, resulting in me pulling her towards one of the doors with everybody watching. She tried to kick me and as I was pulling her she lost her balance and went crashing to the floor. As we were running towards the village, pursued by a swarm of enraged dancers, Alberto lamented all the wine her husband might have bought us.

THE END OF THE ROAD FOR LA PODEROSA II

W E GOT up early to put the finishing touches to the bike and flee what was no longer a very hospitable spot for us, but not before accepting a final invitation to lunch from the family next to the garage.

Alberto had a premonition and didn't want to drive, so I took the controls. We did quite a few kilometres before stopping to fix the gearbox. Not much further on, as we went round a tight bend at quite a speed, the screw came off the back brake, a cow's head appeared round the bend, then lots more, and I clutched the hand brake which, soldered in an elementary fashion, broke too. For a moment I saw nothing but the shapes of cattle flashing by on all sides, while poor Poderosa gathered speed down the steep hill. By an absolute miracle, all we touched was the leg of the last cow. In the distance there was a river which seemed to be beckoning us with terrifying certainty. I steered the bike on to the side of the road and it flew up the two-metre bank, ending up lodged between two rocks, but we were unhurt.

Still reaping the benefit of the letter of recommendation from the press, we were put up by some Germans who treated us very well. During the night I had a bad case of the runs and, not wanting to leave a souvenir in the pot under my bed, I positioned myself at the window and delivered up the contents of my aching guts to the darkness beyond. The next morning I looked out to see the effect and saw that two metres below was a large tin roof with peaches on it drying in the sun; the spectacle added by me was impressive. We beat a speedy retreat.

Although at first the accident hadn't seemed important, it was now clear that we had underestimated it. The bike did strange things every time it had to go uphill. We began the climb to Malleco where there is a railway bridge the Chileans say is the highest in the Americas. The bike packed it in halfway up and we wasted the whole day waiting for some charitable soul in the form of a lorry to take us to the top. We slept in the town of Cullipulli (after the lift materialized) and left early, expecting catastrophe. On the first steep hill – one of many on that road – La Poderosa finally gave up the ghost. A lorry took us to Los Angeles where we left her in the fire station and slept at the house of a Chilean army lieutenant who seemed very grateful for the way he'd been treated in Argentina and couldn't do enough to please us. It was our last day as 'motorized bums'; the next stage, as 'non-motorized bums', looked like being more difficult.

VOLUNTEER FIREMEN, WORKMEN
AND THE LIKE

I N CHILE there are (as far as I'm aware) no non-volunteer fire brigades, but it's still a very good service because captaining a brigade is an honour much sought after by the most able men in the towns or districts where they operate. And don't think it's a job only in theory: in the South at least there are an amazing number of fires. I don't know if you can put it down to the fact that most buildings are made of wood, or that the people are poor and not very well educated, or some other factor, or all of them put together. What I do know is that in the three days we were at the fire station there were two big fires and one little one. (I'm not suggesting this was average, just stating the facts.)

I haven't explained that after spending the night at the lieutenant's house, we decided to move to the fire station, lured by the caretaker's three daughters, prime examples of the charm of Chilean women who, ugly or pretty, have a certain spontaneity and freshness which is immediately captivating. But I digress ... They gave us a room where we put up our camp beds and slept our usual sleep of the dead which meant we didn't hear the sirens. The volunteers on duty didn't know we were there and rushed off with their fire engines while we carried on sleeping until past mid morning, when we learned what had happened. We made them promise to call us for the next fire. We'd already found a lorry to take us and the bike to Santiago in two days' time for a small fee, on condition we helped them with the load of furniture they were moving.

We were a very popular pair and always had lots to chat about with the volunteers and the caretaker's daughters, so the days in Los Angeles simply flew by. In my eyes which insist on categorizing and anecdotizing the past, however, the town is symbolized by the furious flames of a fire. It was the last day of our stay, and after copious libations demonstrating the good mood of the goodbyes, we had curled up in our blankets and gone to sleep when a bell (the one we'd been waiting for) calling duty volunteers ripped through the night – and through Alberto's bed which he sprang out of too quickly. We soon took up our positions with appropriate gravity in the fire engine 'Chile-España' which shot out of the station, the long whine of its alarm siren not alarming anyone, too familiar to be much of a novelty.

A house of wood and adobe shook with each gush of water falling on its flaming skeleton, while the acrid smoke of burnt wood defied the stoical work of the firemen who, roaring with laughter, protected the neighbouring houses with water jets or other means. From the only part of the house the flames hadn't reached came the yowling of a cat which, terrified by the fire, just miaowed and refused to escape through the small space left. Alberto saw the danger, measured it at a glance and, with an agile leap, jumped the twenty centimetres of flames and saved the little endangered life for its owners. As he received effusive congratulations for his peerless courage, his eyes shone with pleasure behind the huge borrowed helmet.

But everything comes to an end and Los Angeles finally bade us farewell. Little Che and Big Che (Alberto and I)[13] gravely

[13] *Che* is commonly used in Argentina to mean 'pal', 'mate', etc. Argentines are often nicknamed Che in other Spanish-speaking countries, hence 'Che' Guevara. The origin could be a Guaraní indian word meaning 'my'; a Mapuche indian word meaning 'man'; or an Andalucían expression.

shook the last friendly hands as the lorry pulled out for Santiago, carrying on its powerful back the corpse of La Poderosa II.

We arrived in Santiago on a Sunday and went straight to the Austin garage. We had a letter of introduction to the owner but found to our dismay that it was closed. We finally got the caretaker to accept the bike, however, and went off to pay for part of the trip with the sweat of our brows.

Our job as porters had different stages: the first, very interesting, took the form of two kilos of grapes each, consumed in record time, helped by the absence of the owners of the house; the second was their arrival and the subsequent hard work; the third, Alberto's discovery that the lorry driver's mate had an exaggerated and misplaced opinion of himself; the poor guy won all the bets we made with him, by carrying more furniture than us and the owner put together (the latter played dumb with great elegance).

Stony-faced (which was fair enough on a Sunday), our consul, who we'd managed to track down, finally turned up at what served as an office and let us sleep in the patio. After haranguing us about our duties as citizens, etc., he outdid himself in generosity by offering us two hundred *pesos* which we, on our high horses, refused. If he'd offered it three months later, it would've been a different story. What a let off!

Santiago looks more or less like Córdoba. The pace of life is quicker and the traffic's much heavier, but the buildings, the streets, the weather and even the people bring to mind our own mediterranean city. We didn't get to know the city well because we were only there a few days and had lots of urgent things to sort out before we took off again.

The Peruvian consul refused to give us a visa without a letter from his Argentine counterpart, and the latter refused because he said the bike probably wouldn't get us there and we'd have to ask the embassy for help (the little angel didn't know the bike was already defunct), but he finally relented and they gave us the visa for Peru, at a fee of four hundred Chilean *pesos*, a hefty sum for us.

Visiting Santiago at the time was the Suquía water-polo team from Córdoba, and many of the lads were friends of ours, so we made a courtesy call on them while they were playing a match and got ourselves invited to one of those 'have some ham, try some cheese, have a little more wine' type Chilean meals that you get up from – if you *can* – straining all the thorax muscles you can muster. Next day, we went up Santa Lucía, a rocky outcrop in the centre of the city with a history all of its own, and were peacefully taking photos of the city when a group of Suquía members arrived shepherded by some beauties from the host club. The poor guys were pretty embarrassed because they didn't know whether to introduce us to these 'distinguished Chilean society ladies', as they eventually did, or pretend not to know us (remember our idiosyncratic attire), but they managed the tricky situation with as much aplomb as possible and were very friendly – as friendly as people could be from worlds as far apart as theirs and ours at that particular moment in our lives.

The big day finally arrived on which two tears ploughed symbolically down Alberto's cheeks and, with one last wave to La Poderosa left in the garage, we set off towards Valparaíso on a magnificent mountain road, the best that civilization can offer compared to real natural wonders (unspoilt by human hand, that is), in a lorry which climbed steadfastly despite our freeloading.

LA GIOCONDA'S SMILE

THIS was a new stage in our adventure. We were used to attracting idle attention with our strange garb and the prosaic figure of La Poderosa II, whose asthmatic wheezing aroused pity in our hosts. All the same, we had been, so to speak, gentlemen of the road. We'd belonged to a time-honoured aristocracy of wayfarers, bearing our degrees as visiting cards to impress people. Not any more. Now we were just two tramps with packs on our backs, and the grime of the road encrusted in our overalls, shadows of our former aristo-cratic selves. The lorry driver had dropped us in the upper part of the city, on the way in, and we wearily dragged our packs down the streets, followed by the amused or indifferent glances of passersby. In the distance, boats glimmered enticingly in the harbour while the sea, black and welcoming, cried out to us with a grey smell which swelled our nostrils. We bought bread – bread which seemed so expensive at the time but proved cheap as we ventured further north – and kept walking down-hill. Alberto was obviously tired, and although I tried not to show it I was just as weary, so when we found a lorry park we besieged the attendant with gruesome details of the hardships we had suffered on the long hard road from Santiago. He let us sleep on some boards, accompanied by parasites whose name ends in hominis, but at least we had a roof over our heads.

Single-mindedly we set about falling asleep. News of our arrival, however, had reached the ears of a fellow-countryman in a scruffy little caff next to the lorry park, and he wanted to meet us. Meeting in Chile means hospitality and neither of us was in a position to turn down this manna from heaven. Our compatriot proved to be deeply imbued with the spirit of the sisterland and was completely pie-eyed. I hadn't eaten fish for ages, and the wine was so delicious, and our host so attentive ... anyway, we ate well and he invited us to his house the following day.

La Gioconda opened its doors early and we brewed our maté, chatting to the owner who was very interested in our journey. After that, we went off to explore the city. Valparaíso is very picturesque. Built overlooking a large bay, as it grew it clambered up the hills which sweep down to the sea. Its strange corrugated-iron architecture, arranged on a series of tiers linked by winding flights of steps and funiculars, has its madhouse museum beauty heightened by the contrast of different-coloured houses mingling with the leaden blue of the bay. As if patiently dissecting, we pry into dirty stairways and dark recesses, talking to the swarms of beggars; we plumb the city's depths, the miasmas to which we are drawn. Our dilated nostrils inhale the poverty with sadistic intensity.

We went to the ships down at the docks to see if any were going to Easter Island but the news wasn't very encouraging: no boats were going there in the next six months. We got some vague details about flights which left once a month.

Easter Island! Our imaginations soar, then stop and circle around: 'Over there, having a white "boyfriend" is an honour'; 'You don't have to work, the women do everything – you just eat, sleep and keep them happy.' This wonderful place where the weather is ideal, the women ideal, the food ideal, the work ideal (in its blissful non-existence). Who cares if we stay there a year, who cares about studying, work, family, etc.? In a shop window an enormous lobster winks at us, and from his bed of lettuce his whole body tells us, 'I'm from Easter Island, where the weather is ideal, the women ideal . . . '

We were waiting patiently in the doorway of La Gioconda for our compatriot to show up, when the owner invited us in out of the sun and treated us to one of his magnificent lunches of fried fish and watery soup. We never heard from the Argentine again while we were in Valparaíso, but we became great friends with the owner of the bar. He was a strange sort of guy, indolent and enormously generous to all the odds and sods who turned up, but he made normal customers pay through the nose for the rubbish he sold in his place. We didn't pay a cent the whole time we were there and he lavished hospitality on us. 'Today it's your turn, tomorrow it'll be mine' was his favourite saying; not very original but very effective.

We tried to contact the doctors from Petrohué, but back at work with no time to waste, they never agreed to meet us formally. At least we knew more or less where they were. That afternoon we went separate ways: Alberto following up the doctors while I went to see an old woman with asthma, a customer at La Gioconda. The poor thing was in an awful state, breathing the smell of stale sweat and dirty feet that filled her room, mixed with the dust from a couple of arm-chairs, the only luxuries in her house. As well as asthma, she had a bad heart. It is in cases like this, when a doctor knows he is powerless in such circumstances, that he longs for change;

a change which would prevent the injustice of a system in which until a month ago this poor old woman had had to earn her living as a waitress, wheezing and panting but facing life with dignity. In these circumstances people in poor families who can't pay their way are surrounded by an atmosphere of barely disguised acrimony; they stop being father, mother, sister or brother and become a purely negative factor in the struggle for life and, by extension, a source of bitterness for the healthy members of the community who resent their illness as if it were a personal insult to those who have to support them. It is then, at the end, for people whose horizons never reach beyond tomorrow, that we see the profound tragedy which circumscribes the life of the proletariat the world over. In these dying eyes there is a humble appeal for forgiveness and also, often, a desperate plea for solace which is lost in the void, just as their body will soon be lost in the vast mystery surrounding us. How long this present order, based on an absurd idea of caste, will last I can't say, but it's time governments spent less time publicizing their own virtues and more money, much more money, funding socially useful projects. There wasn't much I could do for the sick woman. I simply advised her on her diet and prescribed a diuretic and some asthma pills. I had a few dramamine tablets left and I gave them to her. As I went out, I was followed by the old dear's fawning words and the family's indifferent gaze.

Alberto had tracked down the doctor. We had to be at the hospital at nine the following morning. Meanwhile, in La Gioconda's grubby room which serves as kitchen, restaurant, laundry room, dining room and piss-house for sundry cats and dogs, a motley crew of people had gathered: the owner, with his homespun philosophy; Doña Carolina, a helpful old dear who was deaf but left our maté kettle as good as new; a drunk, feeble-minded Mapuche indian who looked like a criminal; two more or less normal clients; and the star of the gathering – Doña Rosita, who was off her rocker. The conversation centred on a macabre event which Rosita had witnessed; it appeared she'd been the only one to see a man with a large knife flaying her poor neighbour.

'Didn't your neighbour scream, Doña Rosita?'

'Of course she screamed, he was skinning her alive! And not only that, afterwards he took her down to the sea and dragged her to the water's edge so the sea would take her away. To hear that woman scream, señor, was heart rending, you should've seen it.'

'Why didn't you tell the police, Rosita?'

'What for? Don't you remember when your cousin was flayed? I went to report it and they told me I was crazy, and if I didn't stop inventing things they'd lock me up, imagine that. No, I'm not telling that lot anything any more.'

The conversation turned to 'God's Messenger', a local man who uses the powers the Lord gave him to cure deafness, dumbness, paralysis, etc., and passes the plate round afterwards. The business seems no worse than any other. The pamphlets are extraordinary and so is people's gullibility, but they quite happily make fun of the things Doña Rosita sees.

The reception from the doctors wasn't over-friendly, but we got what we wanted: an introduction to Molinas Luco, Mayor of Valparaíso. We took our leave with all the required formality and went to the Town Hall. Our scruffy appearance didn't impress the man at the desk, but he'd had orders to let us in.

The secretary showed us the copy of a letter replying to ours, explaining that our project was impossible since the only ship to Easter Island had left and there wasn't another for a year. We were ushered into the sumptuous office of Dr Molinas Luco, who received us very cordially. He gave the impression, however, of being in a play and was very careful with his diction. He only became enthusiastic when he talked about Easter Island, which he had wrested from the English by proving it belonged to Chile. He recommended we keep up with events and promised to take us next year. 'I may not be here exactly, but I'm still President of the Friends of Easter Island Society,' he said, a tacit admission of González Videla's forthcoming electoral defeat. As we went out, the man at the desk told us to take our dog with us, and to our amazement showed us a puppy which had relieved itself on the lobby carpet and was gnawing a chair leg. The dog had probably followed us, attracted by our hobo look, and the doorman had imagined it was just another accessory of our outlandish attire. Anyway, the poor animal, deprived of the bond linking him to us, got a good kick up the bum and was thrown out howling. Still, it was good to know that some living thing's well-being depended on our patronage.

We were determined to avoid the desert in the North of Chile by going by sea, so we went round the shipping companies trying to get a free passage to one of the northern ports. In one of them, the captain promised to take us if the maritime authorities gave us permission to work our passage. The reply was negative, of course, and we were back at square one. Alberto suddenly informed me of his heroic decision: we'd sneak on to the boat and hide in the hold. It would be best to do it at night, persuade the sailor on duty and see what happened. We fetched our bags, clearly too many for this particular plan. After saying goodbye with great regret to our friends, we went through the main gates of the port and, burning our boats, set off on our maritime adventure.

STOWAWAYS

W E GOT through customs with no trouble and headed boldly for our target. The boat we'd chosen, the *San Antonio*, was the centre of feverish activity in the port but, because it was small, it didn't need to come right alongside the quay for the cranes to reach it, so there was a gap of several metres between it and the docks. We had no option but to wait until the boat moved closer before going on board, and we sat on our bundles waiting philosophically for a suitable moment. At midnight, with a change of shift, the boat was brought alongside, but the harbour master, an unfriendly looking fellow, stood squarely on the gangplank checking the men. We'd made friends with the crane driver in the meantime and he advised us to wait for a better moment because the guy was a real bastard. So we began a long wait which lasted all night, keeping warm in the crane, an ancient contraption which ran on steam. The sun came up and we were still with our bundles on the dock. Our hopes of getting aboard had almost vanished when the captain turned up with a ramp which had been being mended, and the *San Antonio* was now permanently connected to dry land. So, given the thumbs up by the crane driver, we slipped on board with no trouble at all and locked ourselves and our bags in a toilet in the officers' quarters. From then on, all we had to do was say in a nasal voice 'Can't come in' or 'Occupied', on the half dozen or so times someone tried to use it.

It was midday and the boat had just sailed, but our good mood was disappearing fast because the toilet, apparently blocked for some time, stank to high heaven and it was incredibly hot. By one o'clock, Alberto had brought up the entire contents of his stomach, and at five in the afternoon, absolutely starving and with no land in sight, we presented ourselves to the captain as stowaways. He was quite surprised to see us again, and in these circumstances, but so as not to let on he knew us in front of the other officers, he winked and thundered: 'D'you think all you have to do to travel is to jump on the first boat you come across? Haven't you thought of the consequences?' The truth is we hadn't given them a moment's thought.

He called the steward and told him to give us work and something to eat. We cheerfully gobbled down our rations, but when I learned I had to clean the famous toilet, the food stuck in my throat. As I went below protesting between clenched teeth, followed by the smirking Alberto, who had been assigned to peeling potatoes, I confess I was tempted to forget everything written about the rules of friendship and ask to change jobs. There's no justice! He adds a fair portion to the accumulated muck and I have to clean it up!

After we'd dutifully done our chores, the captain summoned us again. This time he advised us not to mention our previous meeting, that he'd make sure nothing happened when we got to Antofagasta, where the boat was headed. He gave us the cabin belonging to an officer on leave, and invited us to play canasta and have a drink or two. After a rejuvenating sleep, we got up and gave credence to the saying 'New brooms sweep clean'. We set to work energetically, determined to earn the price of our passage with interest. However, by midday we thought we were overdoing it and by late afternoon we were definitely convinced we were the most inveterate pair of lay-abouts ever. We wanted to get a good sleep, ready for work the next day, not to mention washing our dirty clothes, but the captain invited us to play cards again and that put paid to our good intentions.

It took the steward, an unpleasant type, about an hour to get us up and working. My job was to clean the decks with kerosene; it took me all day and I still hadn't finished. Alberto, cunning bastard, still in the kitchen, ate more and better, not being too fussy about what he was shovelling into his stomach.

At night, after the exhausting games of canasta, we'd lean on the rail and look out over the vast sea, gleaming greeny-white, side by side but each lost in his own thoughts, on his own flight towards the stratosphere of dreams. There we discovered that our vocation, our true vocation, was to roam the highways and waterways of the world for ever. Always curious, investigating everything we set eyes on, sniffing into nooks and crannies; but always detached, not putting down roots anywhere, not stay-ing long enough to discover what lay beneath things: the surface was enough. While all the sentimental nonsense the sea inspires drifted through our conversation, the lights of Antofa-gasta began to wink in the distance, to the north-east. It was

the end of our adventure as stowaways, or at least the end of
this adventure, since our boat was going back to Valparaíso.

THIS TIME, FAILURE

I CAN see him now, clear as day: the drunken captain,
likewise all his officers and the moustachioed owner of the
vessel alongside, their coarse gestures the product of bad wine.
And the raucous laughter as they recounted our odyssey.
'They're tigers, you know, bet they're on your boat now, you'll
find out when you're out at sea.' The captain must have let slip
to his friend this or some similar phrase. We didn't know that,
of course; an hour before sailing we were comfortably installed, buried in tons of sweet-smelling melons, stuffing ourselves silly. We were just saying how great sailors were since
one of them had helped us get on board and hide in such a good
place, when we heard an angry voice, and a moustache, larger
than life, emerged from who knows where and plunged us into
the depths of confusion. A long line of melon skins, scraped
clean, was floating away in indian file on the calm sea. What
followed was ignominious. The sailor told us afterwards, 'I'd
have got him off the scent, lads, but he saw the melons and it
seems he went into a "batten down the hatches, don't let
anyone escape" routine. And well,' (he was sort of embarrassed) 'you shouldn't have eaten all that melon, lads!'

One of our friends from the *San Antonio* summed up his
exquisite philosophy of life with elegant words: 'You're up shit
creek because you're such shits. Why don't you stop shitting

about and shit off back to your shitty country.'[14] So that's more or less what we did; we picked up our bags and set off for Chuquicamata, the famous copper mine.

But not straight away. We had to wait a day for permission from the authorities to visit the mine and meanwhile got the appropriate send-off from enthusiastic Bacchanalian sailors.

Lying in the meagre shade of two lamp-posts on the arid road leading to the mines, we spent a good part of the day yelling things at each other every now and again from one post to another, until we spied the asthmatic shape of the van which took us halfway, to a town called Baquedano.

There we made friends with a married couple, Chilean workers who were Communists.[15] In the light of a candle, drinking maté and eating a piece of bread and cheese, the man's shrunken features struck a mysterious, tragic note. In simple but expressive language he told us about his three months in prison, his starving wife who followed him with exemplary loyalty, his children left in the care of a kindly neighbour, his fruitless pilgrimage in search of work and his comrades who had mysteriously disappeared and were said to be somewhere at the bottom of the sea.

The couple, numb with cold, huddling together in the desert night, were a living symbol of the proletariat the world over. They didn't have a single miserable blanket to sleep under, so we gave them one of ours and Alberto and I wrapped the other

---

[14] 'Shit' has been used instead of the very common Chilean expletive *huevos* (balls). The original reads: '*Están a la hueva de puro huevones. ¿Por qué no se dejan de huevadas y se van a huevear a su huevona tierra?*'

[15] The Chilean Communist Party was proscribed and many militants persecuted under the so-called Law for the Defence of Democracy (1948–58).

round us as best we could. It was one of the coldest nights I've ever spent; but also one which made me feel a little closer to this strange, for me anyway, human species.

At eight the next morning we got a lorry to take us to the town of Chuquicamata. We said goodbye to the couple who were heading for the sulphur mines in the mountains where the weather is so bad and conditions so hard that you don't need a work permit and nobody asks what your politics are. The only thing that counts is the enthusiasm with which the worker ruins his health for a few meagre crumbs.

Although by now we could barely make out the couple in the distance, the man's singularly determined face stayed with us and we remembered his simple invitation: 'Come, comrades, come and eat with us. I'm a vagrant too,' which showed he basically despised our aimless travelling as parasitical.

It's really upsetting to think they use repressive measures against people like these. Leaving aside the question of whether or not 'Communist vermin' are dangerous for a society's health, what had burgeoned in him was nothing more than the natural desire for a better life, a protest against persistent hunger transformed into a love for this strange doctrine, whose real meaning he could never grasp but, translated into 'bread for the poor', was something he understood and, more importantly, that filled him with hope.

The bosses, the blond, efficient, arrogant managers, told us in primitive Spanish: 'This isn't a tourist town. I'll get a guide to give you a half-hour tour round the mine and then please be good enough to leave, we have a lot of work to do.' A strike was in the offing. Yet the guide, the Yankee bosses' faithful lapdog, told us: 'Stupid gringos, they lose thousands of *pesos* every day in a strike so as not to give a poor worker a couple of extra *centavos*. That'll be over when our General Ibañez comes to power.'[16] And a foreman-poet: 'These famous terraces enable every scrap of copper to be mined. People like you ask me lots of technical questions but I'm rarely asked how many lives it has cost. I don't know the answer, doctors, but thank you for asking.'

Cold efficiency and impotent resentment go hand in hand in the big mine, linked despite the hatred by the common need to survive, on the one side, and to speculate on the other ... maybe one day, some miner will joyfully take up his pick and go and poison his lungs with a smile. They say that's what it's like over there, where the red blaze dazzling the world comes from. So they say. I don't know.

CHUQUICAMATA

C HUQUICAMATA is like a scene from a modern play. You can't say it lacks beauty, but it's a beauty which is imposing, charmless and cold. As you approach the mine, the whole landscape creates a feeling of suffocation on the plain. There is one point at which, after two hundred kilometres, the slight greeny hue of the town of Calama interrupting the monotonous grey is greeted with a joy which as an oasis in the desert it

[16] Carlos Ibañez del Campo was President of Chile from 1952 to 1958. He was a populist, who promised to legalize the Communist Party if elected.

richly deserves. And what a desert! The weather observatory at Moctezuma, near 'Chuqui', calls it the driest in the world. The mountains, devoid of a single blade of grass in the nitrate soil, defenceless against the attack of wind and water, display their grey backbone, prematurely aged in the battle with the elements, their wrinkles belying their real geological age. And how many of the mountains surrounding their famous brother hide similar riches deep in their bowels, awaiting the arid arms of the mechanical shovels to devour their entrails, spiced with the inevitable human lives – the lives of the poor unsung heroes of this battle, who die miserable deaths in one of the thousand traps nature sets to defend its treasures, when all they want is to earn their daily bread.

Chuquicamata is essentially a great copper mountain with twenty-metre-high terraces cut into its enormous sides, from where the extracted mineral is easily transported by rail. The unique formation of the vein means that extraction is all open cast, allowing large-scale exploitation of the ore-body which grades 1 per cent copper per ton of ore. The mountain is dynamited every morning and huge mechanical shovels load the material on to rail wagons on which it is taken to the grinder to be crushed. This crushing consists of three stages which turn the raw material into medium-sized gravel. It is then put in a sulphuric acid solution which extracts the copper in the form of sulphate, also forming a copper chloride, which turns into ferrous chloride when it comes into contact with old iron. From there the liquid is taken to the so-called 'green house' where the copper sulphate solution is put into huge baths and submitted to a current of thirty volts for a week which brings about the electrolysis of the salt: the copper sticks to the thin sheets of the same metal, which have previously been formed in other baths with stronger solutions. After five or six days, the sheets are ready for the smelter; the solution has lost eight to ten grammes of sulphate per litre and is enriched with new quantities of the ground material. The sheets are then placed in furnaces which, after twelve hours smelting at two thousand degrees centigrade, produce 350-pound ingots. Every night forty-five wagons in convoy take over twenty tons of copper each down to Antofagasta, the result of a day's work.

This is a crude summary of the manufacturing process which employs a floating population of three thousand souls in Chuquicamata; but this process only extracts oxide ore. The Chile Exploration Company is building another plant to exploit the sulphate ore. This plant, the biggest of its kind in the world, has two 96-metre-high chimneys and will take almost all future production, while the old plant will be slowly phased out since the oxide ore is about to run out. There is already an enormous stockpile of raw material to feed the new smelter and it will start being processed in 1954 when the plant is opened.

Chile produces 20 per cent of all the world's copper, and copper has become vitally important in these uncertain times of potential conflict because it is an essential component of various types of weapons of destruction. Hence, an economico-political battle is being waged in Chile between a coalition of nationalist and left-wing groupings which advocate nationalizing the mines, and those who, in the cause of free enterprise, prefer a well-run mine (even in foreign hands) to possibly less efficient management by the state. Serious accusations have been made in Congress against the companies currently exploiting the concessions, symptomatic of the climate of nationalist aspiration which surrounds copper production.

Whatever the outcome of the battle, it would be as well not to forget the lesson taught by the mines' graveyards, which contain but a fraction of the enormous number of people devoured by cave-ins, silicosis and the mountain's infernal climate.

KILOMETRES AND KILOMETRES OF ARIDITY

WE'D LOST our water bottle, which made the problem of crossing the desert on foot even worse. Still, throwing caution to the wind, we set off, leaving behind the barrier marking the Chuquicamata town limits. We kept up an energetic pace while within sight of the inhabitants, but then the vast solitude of the bare Andes, the sun beating down on our heads, the badly distributed weight of our rucksacks brought us back to reality. How far our actions were, as one policeman put it, 'heroic' we're not sure, but we began to suspect, and with good cause I think, that the definitive adjective was somewhere in the region of 'stupid'.

After two hours' walking, ten kilometres at the most, we settled down in the shade of a sign saying I've no idea what, the only thing capable of giving us the slightest shelter from the sun's rays. And there we stayed all day, shifting around to get the post's shade in our eyes at least.

The litre of water we had brought with us was rapidly consumed and by the evening, our throats parched, we set off back towards the sentry post by the barrier, in abject defeat.

We spent the night there, sheltering inside the little room, where a bright fire kept the temperature pleasant despite the cold outside. The nightwatchman shared his food with us, with the proverbial Chilean hospitality, a meagre feast after a whole day's fasting, but better than nothing.

At dawn the next day a cigarette company's lorry passed and took us in the direction we were heading; but while it was going straight on to the port of Tocopilla, we wanted to go north to Ilave, so it dropped us where the roads crossed. We started walking towards a house we knew was eight kilometres up the road, but halfway there we got tired and decided to have a nap. We hung our blankets between a telegraph post and a distance marker and lay under them, our bodies having a Turkish bath and our feet a sunbathe.

Two or three hours later, when we'd lost about three litres of water each, a small Ford went by with three noble citizens in it roaring drunk and singing *cuecas*[17] at the tops of their voices. They were workers on strike from the Magdalena mine prematurely celebrating the victory of the people's cause by getting merrily plastered. The drunks dropped us at a local railway station. There we found a group of navvies practising for a football match with a rival team. Alberto took a pair of trainers out of his rucksack and started his spiel. The result was spectacular. We were signed up for the following Sunday's match; in return: lodging, food and transport to Iquique.

[17] Chilean folk dances.

It was two days to Sunday which was marked by a splendid victory for our team and some barbecued goats which Alberto cooked, astounding the assembled gathering with Argentine culinary skill. In those two days we visited some of the many nitrate purifying plants in that area of Chile.

It really isn't very difficult for mining companies to extract the mineral wealth of this part of the world. All they have to do is scrape off the top layer, which is where the mineral is, and transport it to huge baths where it goes through a not very complicated separating process to extract the nitrates, saltpetre and mud. The Germans had the first concessions apparently, but their plants were expropriated and now they are mainly British owned. The two biggest in terms of both production and workforce were on strike at the time and were south of where we were heading, so we decided not to visit them. We went instead to quite a big plant, La Victoria, which has a plaque at the entrance marking the spot where Hector Supicci Sedes died. He was a brilliant Uruguayan rally driver who was hit by another driver as he came out of the pit after refuelling.

A succession of lorries took us all over the region until we finally reached Iquique warmly wrapped in a blanket of alfalfa, the cargo of the truck which brought us on the final leg. Our arrival, with the sun coming up behind us reflected in the pure blue of the morning sea, was like something out of the *Thousand and One Nights*. The lorry appeared like a magic carpet on the cliffs above the port, and on our twisting and grumbling flight down, first gear slowing our descent, from our vantage point we saw the whole city come up to meet us.

In Iquique there wasn't a single boat, Argentine or any other

kind, so it was pointless staying in the port and we decided to
cadge a lift on the first lorry to Arica.

CHILE, THE END

T HE LONG kilometres between Iquique and Arica are up and
down all the way. The road took us from arid plateaux to
valleys with trickles of water at the bottom, barely enough for
a few small stunted trees to grow at the edge. During the day
these totally arid plains are oppressively hot but it gets con-
siderably cooler at night, like all desert climates. It's astonish-
ing to think that Valdivia came this way with his handful of
men, travelling fifty or sixty kilometres without finding a drop
of water or even a bush to shelter under at the hottest time of
day. When you actually see the terrain the *conquistadores*
crossed, you automatically raise the feat of Valdivia and his
men to one of the most remarkable of Spanish colonization,
surely greater than those which live on in the history of
America because the men concerned were fortunate enough to
conquer immensely rich kingdoms which turned the sweat of
their bellicose adventure into gold. Valdivia's achievement
symbolizes man's undeniable desire to find a place where
he can exercise absolute control. Those words attributed to
Caesar, when he declared he would rather be number one in a
humble village in the Alps than number two in Rome, find their
echo less bombastically, but no less effectively, in the conquest
of Chile. If when facing death at the hands of the indomitable

Araucanian Caupolicán, the *conquistador*'s last moments had not been clouded by the fury of a hunted animal, I've no doubt that, looking back over his life, Valdivia would have found ample justification for his death in being the supreme ruler of a warrior nation, because he belonged to that special kind of man which races produce every so often, for whom suffering seems a natural price to pay for their sometimes unconscious yearning for limitless power.

Arica is a pleasant little port which still shows traces of its previous owners, the Peruvians, and acts as a sort of halfway house between two countries which are so different despite their geographical contact and common ancestry.

The headland, pride of the town, is a hundred metres of sheer rock face. The palm trees, the heat, the subtropical fruit in the markets, give it the special feel of a Caribbean town, quite different from its counterparts further south.

A doctor, who treated us with all the disdain a staid, financially solid bourgeois feels for a pair of bums (even bums with degrees), let us sleep in the town hospital. We fled the not very hospitable place early and headed straight for the frontier with Peru. But first we said goodbye to the Pacific with one last bathe (soap and all) and it awakened a dormant desire in Alberto: to eat seafood. So we patiently searched for clams and other seafood on the beach by some cliffs. We ate something slimy and salty, but it neither took our minds off our hunger nor assuaged Alberto's craving, and wouldn't have made even a convict happy because the slime was so unpleasant and, with nothing on it, worse.

After eating at the police station, we left at our usual time for the slog along the coast to the frontier. However, a van picked us up and we reached the border post in style. There we met a customs officer who had worked on the frontier with Argentina so he recognized and understood our passion for maté and gave us hot water, biscuits and, better still, a ride to Tacna. With a handshake and a load of pompous platitudes about Argentines in Peru with which the police chief amiably welcomed us at the border, we bade farewell to the hospitable land of Chile.

CHILE, IN RETROSPECT

W HEN I jotted down these notes, in the heat of my early enthusiasm and first impressions, what I wrote included a few wild inaccuracies and was generally not in the approved spirit of scientific inquiry. Anyway, I don't think I should express my current ideas about Chile now, more than a year after I made the notes; I'd rather do a précis of what I wrote then.

Let's start with our medical speciality: health care in Chile generally leaves much to be desired (I realized afterwards that it was much better than in other countries I visited). Totally free hospitals are very few and far between and you see this sort of notice: 'How can you complain about the treatment you receive if you don't contribute to the upkeep of this hospital?' Nevertheless, medical attention in the North is generally free, but hospital accommodation has to be paid for, ranging from derisory sums to virtual monuments to legalized robbery. At the Chuquicamata mine, sick or injured workers get medical attention and hospital treatment for five Chilean *escudos* a day but patients not from the plant pay between 300 and 500 *escudos* a day. Hospitals are generally poor, and lack medicine and adequate facilities. We saw badly lit and even dirty operating rooms, not just in small towns but indeed in Valparaíso. There aren't enough instruments. The toilets are dirty. Sanitary awareness in Chile is poor. Chileans have a custom (which I saw afterwards all over South America) of not throwing used toilet paper in the lavatory but on the floor or in the boxes provided.

The Chileans' standard of living is lower than in Argentina. In the South, wages are very low, unemployment is high and workers get very little protection from the authorities (better, however, than provided in the north of the continent). All this causes waves of Chileans to emigrate to Argentina searching for the proverbial streets paved with gold which clever political propaganda has offered the inhabitants to the west of the Andes. In the North, workers in the copper, nitrate and sulphur mines are better paid, but the cost of living is much higher; they lack many essential consumer goods and the climate in the mountains is very harsh. I remember the eloquent shrug of the shoulders with which a manager of the Chuquicamata mine answered my questions about compensation paid to the families of the ten thousand or more workers buried in the local cemetery.

The political scene is confusing (this was written before the elections which Ibáñez won). There are four presidential candidates, of whom Carlos Ibáñez del Campo seems the most likely winner. He is a retired soldier with dictatorial tendencies and political ambitions similar to those of Perón, and the people see him as a sort of *caudillo*. His power base is the Popular Socialist Party, which is supported by various minor factions. In second place, I think, is Pedro Enrique Alfonso, the official government candidate. His politics are ambiguous; he seems friendly with the Americans and flirts with all the other parties. The standard bearer of the right is Arturo Matte Larraín, a big shot who is the son-in-law of the late President Alessandri and has the support of all the reactionary sectors of the population. And lastly there is Salvador Allende, the Popular Front candidate. He has the support of the Communist Party, but their votes have been reduced by forty thousand, the number of people deprived of the right to vote because of their affiliation to the party.

Ibañez will probably follow a policy of Latinamericanism and play on the hatred of the United States to win popularity, nationalize the copper and other mines (knowing the enormous deposits the US has ready to start production in Peru doesn't make me very confident that nationalizing these mines will be feasible, at least in the short term), continue nationalizing the railways and substantially increase Argentine–Chilean trade.

As a country, Chile offers economic possibilities to anyone willing to work as long as he's not from the proletariat, that is to say, anyone who has a certain amount of education and technical knowledge. The land can sustain enough livestock (especially sheep) to provide for its population and enough cereals. It has the mineral resources to make it a powerful industrial country: iron, copper, coal, tin, gold, silver, manganese, nitrates. The main thing Chile has to do is to get its tiresome Yankee friend off its back, a Herculean task, at least for the time being, given the huge US investment and the ease with which it can bring economic pressure to bear whenever its interests are threatened.

TARATA, THE NEW WORLD

W E WERE only a few metres from the Civil Guard post marking the end of the village, but our rucksacks already felt as if they weighed a ton. The sun beat down and, as usual, we had too many clothes on for the time of day, although later we'd be too cold. The road climbed steeply and we soon passed the pyramid we'd seen from the village, a monument to the Peruvians who died in the war with Chile a century ago.[18] We decided it was a good place to make our first stop and try our luck with passing lorries. In the direction we were heading lay nothing but bare hills, almost devoid of vegetation. Sleepy Tacna, with its narrow dirt roads and terracotta roofs, looked even smaller in the distance. We were thrilled at the sight of our first lorry. We timidly stuck out our thumbs and to our surprise the driver stopped beside us. Alberto took charge of the negotiations, explaining in all too familiar words the purpose of our trip and asking for a lift; the driver agreed and indicated we should climb in the back, with a load of indians.

---

[18] In the so-called 'Nitrate Wars' of 1879–83, Chile annexed the mineral-rich Atacama desert.

Overjoyed, we picked up our bags and were about to climb aboard when he shouted: 'Five *soles*[19] to Tarata, OK?'

Furious, Alberto asked why he'd agreed when we'd asked to be taken free of charge. He didn't know what 'free of charge' meant exactly, but to Tarata it was five *soles* ...

'And they'll all be the same,' Alberto said, venting his anger at me with those simple words because it had been my idea to hitch on the road instead of waiting for the lorries in town as he had suggested. The choice was simple. Either we went back, which meant admitting defeat, or we carried on, come what may. We opted for the latter and started walking. That this was not an altogether wise decision soon became apparent: the sun was about to set and there was absolutely no sign of life. Still, we imagined there must be some hut or other so near the village and, bolstered by this hope, we carried on.

It was soon pitch dark and we hadn't come across any sign of habitation. Worse still, we had no water to cook or make maté with. The cold intensified; the desert conditions and the altitude turned the screw. We were very tired. We decided to spread our blankets on the ground and sleep till dawn. The moonless night was very dark so we groped around spreading our blankets and wrapped ourselves up as best we could.

Five minutes later Alberto said he was frozen stiff and I replied that I was even stiffer. Since this wasn't a fridge competition, we decided to face up to the situation and collect twigs for a fire. The result was predictably pathetic. Between us we managed a handful of twigs which made a timid fire giving off no heat at all. Hunger was one problem but the cold

[19] Peruvian currency.

was even worse, so bad in fact that we could no longer lie there watching our four meagre embers. We had to pack up and walk on in the dark. We set off briskly at first to keep warm but were soon panting for breath. I could feel the sweat pouring off me under my jacket, but my feet were numb with cold and the wind cut our faces like a knife. After a couple of hours we were exhausted; it was still only 12.30 by my watch. The most optimistic reckoning gave us another five hours before dawn. Further deliberations, then another attempt at sleeping in our blankets. Five minutes later we were on our way again. It was still the early hours when a headlamp appeared in the distance; there was no point getting too excited at the chances of being picked up but at least we could see the road. And true enough, the lorry went by, indifferent to our hysterical shouts, while its lights revealed an uninhabited wasteland, not a single tree or house. After that, everything became hazy: the minutes passed more and more slowly until eventually minutes seemed like hours. Two or three times the distant barking of a dog offered some hope, but we couldn't see anything in the pitch black night and the dogs fell silent or were in the wrong direction.

At six in the morning, in the grey light of dawn, we saw two shacks by the roadside. We covered the last few metres in a flash, as if we had nothing on our backs at all. We felt that never had a welcome been so friendly, the bread they sold us with a chunk of cheese never so delicious, nor the maté so invigorating. To these simple people, at whom Alberto flourished his doctor's certificate, we were like demigods, from Argentina no less, that wonderful country where Perón and his wife Evita lived, where the poor have as much as the rich and the indian isn't exploited or treated callously as he is in this country. We had to answer thousands of questions about our country and the life there. With the cold of the night still deep in our bones, Argentina was transformed into an alluring vision of a rose-coloured past. Heartened by the shy kindness of the '*cholos*',[20] we made for a dry riverbed close by where we spread our blankets and slept, caressed by the warmth of the rising sun.

At twelve we set off again, our spirits high, the hardships of the previous night forgotten, following the advice of old Vizcacha.[21] It's a long road, however, and our pauses soon became remarkedly frequent. At five in the afternoon we stopped to rest, noting the silhouette of an approaching lorry with indifference; as usual it was carrying a cargo of human livestock, the most profitable business in those parts. To our surprise, the lorry stopped and we saw the civil guard from Tacna giving us a friendly wave and inviting us to climb aboard; naturally we didn't need asking twice. The Aymará indians in the back stared at us with curiosity without daring to ask anything. Alberto talked to some of them, but their Spanish was very poor. The lorry continued climbing through a landscape of utter desolation where only a few straggling thorn bushes gave any semblance of life. Then, suddenly, the lorry's laboured whine as it trundled its way uphill gave way to a sigh of relief as we levelled out on to the plateau. We came to the town of Estaque and the view was wonderful; we gazed, enchanted, at

[20] Indians or mestizos.
[21] A Polonius-like character from *Martín Fierro*, an epic poem of gaucho life by the Argentine José Hernández.

the landscape spreading out before us and wanted to know the names and explanations for everything we saw. The Aymarás barely understood us but the little information they gave in their jumbled Spanish added to the impact of the surroundings. We were in an enchanted valley where time had stopped several centuries ago, and which we lucky mortals, until then stuck in the twentieth century, had been given the good fortune to see. The irrigation channels – which the Incas built for the benefit of their subjects – flowed down the valley, forming a thousand waterfalls and criss-crossing the road as it spiralled down the mountainside. Ahead of us, low clouds covered the mountain tops, but through gaps here and there you could see snow falling on the highest peaks, gradually turning them white. The various crops grown by the indians, neatly cultivated on terraces, opened up a whole new range of botanical science to us: *oca, quinua, canihua, rocoto*, maize. People dressed like the indians sharing our lorry now appeared in their natural habitat, in short dull-coloured woollen ponchos, tight calf-length trousers, and sandals made from rope or old tyres. Avidly drinking in all these sights, we continued down the valley to Tarata. In Aymará this means junction, or place of confluence, aptly named since it stands at the end of a huge V formed by the mountain chains guarding it. It is an ancient, peaceful town where life goes on much the same as it has for centuries. Its colonial church must be an archaeological gem because as well as being very old it combines imported European art with the spirit of the local indians. Narrow streets on many different levels, paved in local stone, indian women carrying their children on their backs ... in short, with so many typical sights, the town conjures up the days before the Spanish Conquest. But the people are not the same proud race that time after time rose up against Inca rule and forced them to maintain a permanent army on their borders; these people who watch us walk through the town streets are a defeated race. They look at us meekly, almost fearfully, completely indifferent to the outside world. Some give the impression that they go on living simply because it's a habit they can't give up. The civil guard took us to the police station where they gave us a bed and some of them invited us to eat. We went for a walk round town and then to bed for a while since we were leaving at three in the morning for Puno on a passenger truck, which was taking us for free thanks to the civil guard.

IN THE REALMS OF PACHAMAMA

BY THREE in the morning the Peruvian police blankets had proved their worth by reviving us with their warmth, when we were shaken awake by the policeman on duty and sadly forced to leave them behind as we set off on the lorry heading for Ilave. It was a magnificent night, but bitterly cold. As a special privilege we were given some planks to sit on which separated us from the smelly, flea-ridden human cargo giving off a heady but warm stench beneath us. When the lorry began to climb, we realized the full extent of the privilege: not a whiff reached our nostrils and no flea could possibly be athletic enough to jump up to our refuge, but on the other hand the wind whipped round our bodies and within minutes we were literally frozen stiff. The lorry kept climbing, so the cold got more and more intense. We had to keep our hands outside the relative protection of our blankets to stop ourselves falling off; the slightest movement would have sent us headlong into the back of the lorry. It was nearly dawn when the lorry stopped because of some carburettor problem which afflicts all engines at this altitude; we were near the highest point of the road, close to five thousand metres. The sun was coming up and a faint light replaced the total darkness we'd travelled in until then. The sun has an odd psychological effect: it had still not come up over the horizon yet we already felt comforted, just thinking about the warmth it would bring.

On the side of the road a huge semi-circular fungus was growing – the only vegetation in the area. We used it to make a pitiful fire, just enough to heat water from a little snow. The spectacle of us two drinking our strange brew must have seemed as interesting to the indians as their typical dress did to us because they kept coming up and asking in their broken Spanish why we were putting water in that peculiar artefact. The lorry flatly refused to take us any further, so we all had to walk about three kilometres in the snow. It was amazing to see how the indians' calloused feet trod the ground without it seeming to bother them, while our toes were completely frozen despite our boots and woolly socks. At their weary steady pace, they trotted along in single file like a string of llamas.

Having got over its nasty turn, the lorry set off with renewed zest and we soon crossed the pass, where there was a strange cairn of irregular stones with a cross on top. As the lorry passed, almost everyone spat and a few made the sign of the cross. Intrigued, we asked what this strange ritual meant but were met with total silence.

The sun was warming up and the temperature rose as we descended, following the course of a river whose source we had seen at the top of the mountain and which had now grown to a fair size. Snow-covered peaks looked down on us all around and herds of llamas and alpacas watched impassively as the lorry drove past, while the occasional shy vicuña fled from the intruder.

During one of our many stops, an indian came shyly over to us with his son who spoke good Spanish and began asking us all about the wonderful 'land of Perón'. Our imaginations fired by the amazing scenery we were passing through, it was easy for us to describe extraordinary events, embellish the exploits of 'the Chief' as our fancy took us, and amaze our listeners with tales of the idyllic beauty of life in our country.

The man got his son to ask us for a copy of the Argentine Constitution with its declaration of rights for old people, and we promised enthusiastically to send him one. When we set off again, the man pulled a delicious-looking cob of corn from under his poncho and offered it to us. We put paid to it pretty quickly, dividing the grains out democratically between us.

Halfway through the afternoon, with the grey leaden sky bearing down on us, we passed a strange place where erosion had transformed the enormous boulders at the side of the road into feudal castles with battlements, gargoyles staring out disconcertingly, and a host of fabulous monsters which seemed to be guarding the place, making sure the mythical characters who inhabited it were left alone. The drizzle which had lashed our faces for some time got stronger and soon turned into a real downpour. The driver called the 'Argentine doctors' and invited us into his cabin, the height of luxury in those parts. We immediately made friends with a schoolteacher from Puno, who had been sacked by the government for being a member of the APRA party.[22] This meant nothing to us, but the man also had indian blood and was extremely well versed in indigenous customs and culture and regaled us with a thousand stories and reminiscences of his life as a schoolteacher. True to his indian blood, he had sided with the Aymarás in the interminable debate by students of the region, against the *Coyas* whom he called wily and cowardly. He also provided us with the key to our travelling companions' strange behaviour earlier in the day. Apparently indians deposit all their sorrows in the form of a symbolic stone in Pachamama, or Mother Earth, when they reach the top of a mountain; these gradually accumulate to form a cairn like the one we saw. Well, when the Spaniards conquered the region, they immediately tried to stamp out this belief and destroy the ritual, but all to no avail. So the monks decided to accept the inevitable and simply place a cross on each pile of stones. All this took place four centuries ago (indeed Garcilaso de la Vega [23] tells the story) and judging by the number of indians who crossed themselves, the monks didn't have much success. With modern means of transport, the faithful now spit out chewed coca instead of placing a stone, and this carries their troubles to rest with Pachamama.

The teacher's voice took on a strange inspired resonance whenever he spoke about his indians, the formerly rebellious

[22] American Popular Revolutionary Alliance, founded in 1930 by Victor Raúl Haya de la Torre.
[23] The Inca Garcilaso as he was known, the son of an Inca princess and a *conquistador*, was one of the chroniclers of the Conquest.

Aymará race who had held the Inca armies at bay, and it switched to deep despondency when he spoke of the indians' present condition, brutalized by modern civilization and the impure mestizos, his bitter enemies, who take revenge on the Aymarás for their own position as neither fish nor fowl. He spoke of the need to set up schools which would help individuals value their own world, enable them to play a useful role within it; of the need to change completely the present system of education which, on the rare occasions it does offer indians an education (education, that is, according to the white man's criteria), only fills them with shame and resentment, leaving them unable to help their fellow indians and at a tremendous disadvantage in a white society which is hostile to them and doesn't want to accept them. The fate of these unhappy people is to vegetate in some obscure bureaucratic job and die hoping that, thanks to the miraculous power of the drop of Spanish blood in their veins, one or other of their children will somehow achieve the goal to which they aspire until the end of their days. As he spoke, the convulsive clenching of his fist betrayed the spirit of a man tormented by his own misfortune and also the very desire he attributed to his hypothetical example. Wasn't he in fact a typical product of an education which damages the person who is granted it as a favour to demonstrate the magic power of that precious 'drop of blood', even if it came from some poor mestizo woman sold to a local *cacique* or was the result of an indian maid's rape by her drunken Spanish master?

Our journey was almost over and the teacher fell silent. The road curved and crossed a bridge over a wide river we had first seen as a stream early that morning. We had reached Ilave.

THE LAKE OF THE SUN

W E COULD only see a small part of the sacred lake's great beauty because the headlands surrounding the bay where Puno lies hid the rest from us. Here and there, reed canoes bobbed up and down in the calm waters and a few fishing boats headed out into the lake. The wind was very cold and the heavy leaden sky mirrored our state of mind. Although we had got to Puno without stopping in Ilave and had been given temporary accommodation and a good meal at the local barracks, our luck now seemed to have run out. The commanding officer had very politely shown us the door, saying that this was a frontier post and it was strictly forbidden for foreign civilians to stay overnight.

But we didn't want to leave without exploring the lake, so we went to the quay to see if anyone would help us appreciate its magnitude from a boat. We had to use an interpreter for the operation because none of the fishermen, all pure Aymará, knew any Spanish at all. For the modest sum of five *soles*, we managed to get them to take us and the officious guide who had now attached himself to us. We even considered swimming in the lake, but thought better of it when we tested the temperature with the tips of our little fingers (Alberto went through the ritual of taking his boots and clothes off, only to put them back on again, of course).

A number of islands emerged in the distance, scattered dots in the immense grey expanse of water. Our guide told us about the fishermen who live there, some of whom had hardly ever seen a white man, and who live according to age-old customs, eating the same food and fishing with the same methods they used five hundred years ago, and preserving their costumes, rituals and traditions intact.

When we got back to the port, we walked over to one of the ferries which run between Puno and a Bolivian port, to try and replenish our depleted stock of maté. But it's not drunk very much in the northern part of Bolivia, in fact they'd barely heard of it, so we couldn't get even half a kilo. We looked over this boat which was designed in England and assembled here; the luxury of it contrasted with the general poverty we'd seen in the region.

Our lodging problem was solved at the Civil Guard post, where a friendly lieutenant put us up in the infirmary, two in one bed but nice and warm at least. The next day, after a fairly interesting visit to the cathedral, we found a lorry going to Cuzco. The doctor in Puno gave us letter of introduction for a Dr Hermosa who had worked with lepers and now lived in Cuzco.

JOURNEY TO THE NAVEL OF THE WORLD

T HE FIRST part of the journey was not very long as the driver dropped us off in Juliaca, where we had to find another lorry heading north. On the recommendation of the Civil Guard in Puno, we made for the police station where we found a sergeant, pissed to the gills, who took a liking to us and invited us for a drink. He ordered beer which everyone downed in one, except for me.

'What's the matter, my Argentine friend, don't you drink?'

'It's not that, but in Argentina we're not used to drinking like this. Don't get me wrong, but we only drink with food.'

'But, *che-e-e*,' he said, prolonging our onomatopoeic patronymic into a nasal whine, 'why didn't you say so?' And with a clap of his hands he ordered some good old cheese sandwiches which went down very well. Then he got carried away with boasting about his exploits and began telling us how everyone in the area was afraid of him because he was such a fabulous shot.

To prove it he pulled out his gun and waved it at Alberto, saying: 'Look, *che-e-e*, stand back twenty metres with a cigarette in your mouth and if I don't light it for you first go, I'll give you fifty *soles*.' Alberto's not that keen on money, he wasn't about to get out of his chair for only fifty *soles*. 'I'll make it a hundred.' Still no sign of interest from Alberto.

By the time he got to two hundred *soles* – on the table, no less – there was a gleam in Alberto's eye, but his instinct for self-preservation was stronger and he didn't move. So the sergeant took off his cap and, aiming at it in a mirror, threw it in the air behind him and fired. The cap remained intact, of course, but the wall didn't and the owner of the bar blew her top and went to the police station to complain.

A few minutes later an officer turned up to find out what was going on and hauled the sergeant off into a corner to give him a talking to. When they came back to our group, the sergeant said to Alberto, making faces at him so he'd get the gist: 'Hey, Argentine, got another banger like the one you just let off?' Alberto caught on and said with all the innocence in the world that he had run out. The officer warned him about letting off fireworks in public places, then told the owner the incident was closed, that no shot had been fired, he couldn't see any trace on the wall. The woman was about to ask the sergeant to move a couple of centimetres from where he was standing stiffly against the wall, but after a quick mental calculation of pros and cons decided to keep her mouth shut and give Alberto an extra telling off.

'These Argentines think they own the place,' she said, adding a few more insults which were lost in the distance as we fled, one of us thinking ruefully of the beer we were missing, the other of the sandwiches.

In the next lorry, we travelled with a couple of youngsters from Lima bent on proving their superiority over the silent indians, who put up with their taunts as if they hadn't heard. At first we looked the other way and tried to ignore them, but what with the tedium of the journey on an unending plain, after several hours we were forced into conversation with the only other white people on board, the only people we could talk to since the wary indians offered barely more than monosyllabic replies to questions from outsiders. In fact, these kids from Lima were normal enough, they just wanted to make clear the difference between them and the indians. Soon a flood of tangos descended on our unsuspecting companions as we chewed energetically on the coca leaves which our new-found friends obligingly obtained for us.

As the light was fading, we reached a village called Ayaviry, where we were put up in a hotel paid for by the head of the Civil Guard. 'What, two Argentine doctors sleeping rough because they have no money? I won't hear of it,' he replied when we feebly protested at his unexpected generosity. But despite the warm bed, neither of us slept a wink: the coca wreaked its revenge on us with waves of nausea, diarrhoea and migraine.

Early next morning, we left in the same lorry for Sicuani where we arrived in mid afternoon after hours of cold, rain and hunger. As usual we spent the night at the Civil Guard post and as usual we were well looked after. A wretched little river called the Vilcanota runs through Sicuani, and we would be following its waters, diluted by oceans of mud, on the next lap of our journey.

We were in the market at Sicuani gazing at the wonderful range of colours overflowing from the stalls, blending with the monotonous cries of the vendors and the monotone hum of the crowd, when we noticed people gathering on a corner and went off to investigate.

A silent crowd surrounded a procession led by a dozen monks in colourful habits who were followed by a few village notables in black suits and suitably mournful faces carrying a coffin. This marked the end of the formal cortège and the start of a mass of people following in a noisy, disorderly throng. The procession halted and one of the black-suited men came out on to a balcony with some sheets of paper in his hand: 'It behoves us, in this moment of farewell to this worthy man so-and-so ... ' After this interminable waffling, the procession moved on another block, then stopped again and another person in black emerged on a balcony. 'So-and-so is dead, but the memory of his good deeds, of his unblemished integrity ...' etc. And so, poor old so-and-so went on his way to that well-known final resting place, pestered by his fellow villagers who unburdened their loathing in this flood of oratory on every corner.

Then, after another day's travelling much like the previous ones, at last: CUZCO!

THE NAVEL OF THE WORLD

THE ONLY word to sum up Cuzco adequately is evocative. An impalpable dust of other ages covers its streets, rising in clouds like a muddy lake when you disturb the bottom. But there are two or three different Cuzcos, or rather, two or three ways in which the city can be evoked. When Mama Occllo dropped her golden wedge and it sank effortlessly into the soil, the first Incas knew this was the place Viracocha had picked as the permanent home for his chosen people who had abandoned their nomadic existence to come as conquerors to their promised land. Nostrils flaring in their zeal for new horizons, they saw their formidable empire grow and their eyes looked beyond the feeble barrier of the surrounding mountains. As the former nomads expanded Tawantinsuyu, they fortified the centre of the lands they had conquered, the navel of the world – Cuzco.[24] To defend this centre they built the massive Sacsahuamán, which dominates the city from its heights, protecting the palaces and temples from the fury of the empire's enemies. This is the Cuzco whose plaintive voice is heard in the fortress

[24] Mama Occllo was the sister/wife of Manco Capac, the first Inca Emperor. According to the legend, the two were born simultaneously, arising from Lake Titicaca, thus symbolizing the unity and equality of the masculine and the feminine. Viracocha was the Inca Creator–God. Tawantinsuyu (meaning four quarters) was the Inca world of which Cuzco was the centre.

destroyed by the stupidity of illiterate Spanish *conquistadores*, in the violated, ruined temples, in the looted palaces, in the brutalized indians. This Cuzco invites you to turn warrior and, club in hand, defend freedom and the life of the Inca. But there is another Cuzco which can be seen from above, displacing the ruined fortress: the Cuzco of red-tiled roofs, its gentle harmony broken by the cupola of a baroque church, the Cuzco seen in the narrow streets as you walk down, the native people in their traditional costumes, all the local colours. This Cuzco invites you to become a reluctant tourist, to glance at things superficially and enjoy yourself under the beauty of a leaden wintry sky. And there is yet another Cuzco, a vibrant city which bears witness to the formidable courage of the soldiers who conquered this region in the name of Spain, expressed in their monuments, the museums and libraries, in the decoration of its churches and in the distinctive features of the white leaders who still take pride in the Conquest. This Cuzco invites you to don armour and, astride a sturdy powerful steed, cleave a path through the defenceless flesh of a flock of naked indians whose human wall crumbles and falls under the four hooves of the galloping beast. Each of these Cuzcos can be admired on its own, and we spent part of our stay looking at each of them.

THE LAND OF THE INCAS

C uzco is completely surrounded by mountains which present as much of a danger for its inhabitants as a defence. To defend themselves, the Incas built the huge fortress of

Sacsahuamán. At least that's the generally accepted version, version I can't dispute for obvious reasons. It could be, however, that the fortress was actually the original centre of the city. During the time immediately after they'd abandoned their nomadic life, when they were still just an ambitious tribe and defence against a numerically superior adversary lay in protecting the settled population, the walls of Sacsahuamán offered the ideal place. This double function of city-fortress explains some of the mysteries of its construction which don't make sense if it was simply meant to repel the invader, plus the fact that Cuzco was left defenceless on all its other sides – although it's worth noting that the fortress is situated so that it controls the two steep valleys leading to the city. The serrated walls mean that, when enemies attack, they can be fought from three sides, and if they penetrate this line of defence, they come up against a similar kind of wall and then a third. This gives the defenders room for manoeuvre and enables them to concentrate on their counter-attack. All this, together with the city's subsequent glory, suggests that the Quechua warriors were undefeated in their defence of their fortress. Even though the fortifications obviously reflect a highly inventive people, well versed in mathematics, they seem – to me, at least – to belong to the pre-Inca stage of their civilization, before they learned to appreciate material comforts, because although architecture and the applied arts were never of pre-eminent importance for a sober race like the Quechuas, they did achieve interesting expression in these fields. Continuing Quechua successes in war drove the enemy tribes further and further from Cuzco, and so they left the confines of the fortress, which in any case became too small for their growing numbers, and spread down the neighbouring valley along the stream whose waters they used. Conscious of their glorious present, they began looking to the past for an explanation of their superiority and that is why, to honour the god whose omnipotence made them the dominant people in the region, they created the temples and the priest caste. Quechua greatness was expressed in stone and so the imposing Cuzco which the Spaniards conquered gradually took shape.

Even today, when the bestial rage of the uncouth conquerors is seen in every action they took to consolidate the Conquest, and the Inca caste has long since disappeared as the dominant power, their blocks of stone are pervaded with a mysterious strength, untouched by the ravages of time. When the Spanish troops sacked the defeated city, they unleashed their fury on the Inca temples, adding to their greed for the gold adorning the walls in precise symbols of Inti the Sun God the sadistic pleasure of exchanging this joyous and life-giving symbol of a sad people for the sorrowful idol of a joyful people. The temples to Inti were razed to their foundations or their walls used to build the churches of the new religion. The cathedral was constructed on the remains of a great palace, while the walls of the Temple of the Sun served as a base for the Church of Santo Domingo, a lesson and a punishment from the proud conqueror. And yet, the heart of America, trembling with indignation, still twitches the docile back of the Andes every now and then, sending huge shock waves up to the surface. The dome of proud Santo Domingo has come crashing down three times to the roar of broken bones and its walls have tottered, cracked and fallen too. But the foundation they were built on, the grey stone block of the Temple of the Sun, remains impervious, and however great the disaster befalling the usurper, not one of its huge rocks shifts.

Kon's revenge, however, is nothing compared to the magnitude of the outrage. The grey stones have grown weary imploring their gods to destroy the hated race of conquerors and now they show no more than the fatigue of inanimate objects, fit only for the admiring cries of some tourist or other. What use was the patient labour of the indians who built the palace of Inca Roca, subtly shaping the edges of the stone, when confronted with the violent energy of the white *conquistador* and his knowledge of bricks, vaulting and rounded arches?

The indian, anxiously awaiting his gods' terrible vengeance, instead saw clouds of churches rising to the sky, suffocating even the possibility of a proud past. The six-metre walls of the Palace of Inca Roca, which the *conquistadores* used as foundations for their colonial palaces, reflect in their perfect form the lament of the defeated warrior.

But the race which created *Ollantay* [25] left more than the city of Cuzco as a memorial to their past glory. For a hundred kilometres along the River Vilcanota or Urubamba there are remains of the Inca past. The most important are on the mountain tops, where their fortresses were impregnable and safe from surprise attack. After two long hours' climb up a narrow mountain track we reached the summit of Pisac. But long before us, the sword of the Spanish soldier had also reached here, destroying its defenders, its defences and its temple. From the scattered stones, you can imagine how the

---

[25] An epic drama of the Inca General Ollanta, who was put to death for falling in love with an Inca princess.

defences were arranged, the site of the Intiwatana, where the noonday sun was 'tied down', and the priests' dwellings. But so little of it remains!

Following the course of the Vilcanota, bypassing some less important sites, we came to Ollantaytambo, the vast fortress which resisted the troops of Hernando Pizarro when Manco II[26] rose up against the Spaniards to found the minor dynasty of the four Incas who coexisted with the Spanish Empire until its last effeminate representative was put to death in the main square in Cuzco on the orders of Viceroy Toledo.

A rocky outcrop more than a hundred metres high drops vertically to the Vilcanota. The fortress is built on the top and its only vulnerable side, which is linked to the neighbouring hills by narrow paths, is also defended by stone structures which prevent easy access by an attacking force comparable in numbers to the defenders. The lower part is purely defensive, the less steep areas being divided into about twenty easily defendable terraces which make the attacker vulnerable to counter-attack from the sides. The soldiers' quarters occupied the upper part of the fortress, which is crowned by a temple that probably contained all their treasures, in the form of objects made of precious metals. But now not even the memory remains and even the enormous blocks which made up the temple have been taken away.

On the road back to Cuzco, near Sacsahuamán, there is a typical Inca terrace which, according to our guide, was where

---

[26] Put on the Inca throne by Francisco Pizarro after helping to unseat Atahualpa, Manco II in turn fought the Spaniards. His first rebellion was crushed at Ollantaytambo in 1536.

the Incas bathed. I found this rather strange, given how far it is from Cuzco, unless it was a ritual form of bathing for the monarch. Anyway (if this version is true) ancient Inca emperors must have had even tougher skins than their descendants because the water, while tasting delicious, is bitterly cold. The site, with three trapezoidal niches on the top (the form and function of which have yet to be explained), is called Tambomachay and is at the entrance to the Valley of the Incas.

But the site which archaeologically and touristically outweighs all others in the region is Machu Picchu. In the local language this means 'old mountain', a name in no way connected with the place which sheltered the last survivors of a free people within its walls. Bingham, the archaeologist who discovered the ruins, thought that rather than a last refuge against the invaders, this was where the dominant Quechua race originally came from and a holy place for them. It was only later, during the Spanish Conquest, that it also became a refuge for the defeated forces. At a cursory glance, several things suggest the American archaeologist was right. In Ollantaytambo, for instance, the most important defence constructions look away from Machu Picchu, even though the slope behind is not steep enough for the defenders to feel secure against attack from there, which suggests they felt they had their backs covered in that direction. Another indication is their obvious concern to keep the site hidden from outsiders, even after all resistance had been crushed. The last Inca himself was captured far from Machu Picchu, where Bingham found almost only female skeletons, which he described as being those of virgins of the Temple of the Sun, a religious order the Spaniards never managed to uncover. Crowning the city, as in most constructions of this type, is the Temple of the Sun with its famous Intiwatana. It is cut from the rock which forms its pedestal, and a succession of carefully polished stones indicate that this is a very important place. Looking out over the river are three windows in the trapezoid form typical of Quechua architecture, which Bingham, somewhat fancifully in my view, identified as the three windows from which the Ayllus brothers of Inca mythology came to the outside world to show the chosen people the way to their promised land. Needless to say, this interpretation has been challenged by many prestigious researchers, and there is also debate about the function of the Temple of the Sun which Bingham claimed was a circular-shaped room, similar to the Temple of the Sun in Cuzco. Whatever the truth, the shape and careful cutting of the stones prove it was an important construction, and it is thought that beneath the huge stones which form its base lies the tomb of the Inca or Incas.

You can see here the difference between the various social classes in the town, as each of them occupied a distinct place according to category, more or less independent from the rest. It is a shame that they only had straw roofs since this meant that no trace of any roofing remains, even on the most luxurious buildings. But it was extremely difficult for architects without knowledge of vaulting or rounded arches to resolve this problem. In the buildings reserved for the soldiers, we were shown a kind of recess in the stones, like a portico, on each side of which there was a hole just big enough for a man's arm. This was apparently a place of punishment; the victim was forced to put both arms through the holes and was then pushed backwards until his bones broke. I wasn't very convinced and stuck my arms in the holes as indicated. Alberto gave me a gentle push and I immediately felt an excruciating pain and thought I'd be torn apart if he continued pressing my chest.

The most impressive view of the whole fortress is from Huayna Picchu (young mountain) which rises a further two hundred metres. This must have been used as a lookout post rather than a residence or a fortress because the buildings are not very significant. Machu Picchu is impregnable on two sides, defended by a three-hundred-metre drop to the river and a narrow gorge which connects to the 'young mountain'; its most vulnerable side is protected by a row of terraces which make any assault hazardous, while to the front, which faces roughly south, massive fortifications and the narrowing of the hilltop make it difficult to attack. And if you remember that the fast-flowing Vilcanota runs round the base of the mountain, it is clear that the first inhabitants of Machu Picchu made a wise choice.

It doesn't really matter, anyway, what the origin of the fortress was, or rather it is best to leave that debate to the archaeologists. The undeniable thing, the most important thing, is that we have before us a pure expression of the most powerful indigenous race in the Americas, untouched by contact with the conquering civilization, and full of immensely evocative treasures in its walls, walls which have died from the boredom of no longer being. The magnificent scenery around it provides the ideal backdrop to inspire the dreams of anyone strolling through its ruins; North American tourists, hidebound by their practical view of the world, can place those representatives of the fallen people they have seen on their journey in among these once-living walls, unaware of the moral distance separating them, since only the semi-indigenous spirit of the South American can grasp the subtle differences.

OUR LORD OF THE EARTHQUAKES

F OR THE first time since the recent earthquake the María Angola was being rung. According to tradition, this famous bell, among the largest in the world, has twenty-seven kilos of gold in it. It was apparently donated by a lady called María Angulo, but the name was changed for reasons of euphony.[27]

The cathedral belltowers, destroyed in the 1950 earthquake, had been restored by General Franco's government, and as a token of gratitude the band was ordered to strike up the Spanish national anthem. As the first notes sounded, the bishop's red hat turned an even deeper red as he waved his arms in the air like a puppet. 'Stop, stop, there has been a mistake,' he cried, while a Spaniard exclaimed indignantly, 'Two years' work, and that's what they play!' Intentionally or not, the band had struck up the Spanish Republican anthem.

In the afternoon, Our Lord of the Earthquakes comes out of his resting place in the cathedral. It is a darkly painted image of Christ, which is paraded through the city, stopping at all the main churches. As it passes, a crowd of layabouts competes to throw handfuls of a little flower which grows profusely on the

[27] Because it rhymed with *culo* (arse in Spanish).

nearby mountain slopes and which the natives call *nucchu*. The vivid red of the flowers, the deep bronze of the Lord of the Earthquakes and the silver of the altar on which he is carried give the procession the air of a pagan festival. The effect is heightened by the multicoloured clothes of the indians, who put on their best traditional costumes as an expression of a culture and way of life which still boasts living values. In contrast, a group of indians in European clothes carries banners at the head of the procession. Their resigned, prim features reflect those Quechuas who turned a deaf ear to Manco II's call and joined Pizarro, stifling their once proud and independent race by the degradation of defeat.

Towering above the groups of small indians gathered to see the procession pass by, you can occasionally glimpse the blond head of a North American, who with his camera and sports shirt seems like (and in fact is) an emissary from another world in this lost corner of the Inca Empire.

HOME TO THE VICTORS

THE ONCE splendid capital of the Inca Empire kept much of its lustre for many years out of simple inertia. New men paraded its riches, but the riches were the same. For some time they were not merely conserved but increased, thanks to the gold and silver mines opened up in the region; except that Cuzco was no longer the navel of the world but just another point on its periphery and the treasure emigrated to new places over the sea to adorn another imperial court. The indians no longer worked the barren earth with the same devotion and the *conquistadores* had certainly not come to eke out a living from the land, but to make an easy fortune by heroic deeds or simple greed. Cuzco's glory gradually faded, pushed to the sidelines, lost in the mountains, while on the Pacific coast its new rival, Lima, grew in importance on the taxes levied by intermediaries on the wealth flowing out of Peru. Although nothing cataclysmic marked the transition, the brilliant Inca capital gradually became what it is now, a relic of bygone days. Only recently has the odd modern building gone up, disturbing the architectural harmony, but otherwise all the monuments of colonial splendour are still intact.

The cathedral is right in the centre of the city. The rough exterior, typical of that era, makes it look more like a fort than a church. Inside, the glitter reflects its glorious past; the huge paintings on the side walls do not compare with the riches contained in the sanctuary but none the less they are not out of place, and a Saint Christopher emerging from the water seemed to me quite a fine piece. The earthquake took its toll there as well: the frames of the paintings are broken and the paintings themselves scratched and wrinkled. The golden frames and the doors to the side altars, also gold and hanging crooked on their hinges, give a strange impression, as if showing the pustules of old age. Gold doesn't have the same quiet dignity as silver which acquires new charm as it ages, and the side walls of the cathedral look like an over-painted old crone. The real artistic prize goes to the wooden choir stalls, carved by indian or mestizo craftsmen. The cedarwood carvings depict scenes from the lives of the saints and blend the spirit of the Catholic Church with the enigmatic soul of the inhabitants of the Andes.

One of the gems of Cuzco, deservedly on every tourist itinerary, is the pulpit of the Basilica of San Blas. It is the only thing of note there but it certainly merits taking the time to admire the fine carving which, like the cathedral choir stalls, shows the fusion of two races, enemies but somehow almost complementary. The entire city is one immense showcase: the churches, of course, but every house, every balcony in every street, evokes times past. Not all of them have the same merit, of course. But as I write, so far away from there, from notes which now seem artificial and colourless, I find it hard to say what impressed me most. Out of the haze of churches I visited, I remember the plaintive image of the Chapel of Belén. Its twin belltowers toppled by the earthquake, it lay like a dismembered animal on the hillside.

In fact, there are very few individual works of art which bear close inspection, you don't go to Cuzco to admire this or that in particular. It's the city as a whole which exudes the calm, but sometimes rather uncomfortable, sensation of a civilization which is dead and gone.

CUZCO IN A NUTSHELL

I F EVERYTHING in Cuzco were wiped from the face of the earth and a small town with no history appeared in its place, there would still be something to say about it. We mixed all our impressions together, like a cocktail. The fortnight we spent there still had that 'bumming' aspect characteristic of the rest of our trip. Our letter of introduction to Dr Hermosa turned out to be quite useful, although he wasn't the kind of man who needed a formal introduction to help you out. It was enough for him to know Alberto had worked with Dr Fernández, one of the most eminent leprologists in the Americas, and Alberto played the card with his usual skill. Long talks with Dr Hermosa gave us an overall picture of life in Peru and the chance to visit the Valley of the Incas in his car. He was very kind to us and also got us a ticket on the train to Machu Picchu.

The average speed of trains from Cuzco is about ten to twenty kilometres an hour because they are in a rickety state and have to cope with steep ascents and descents. In addition, in order to leave the city, the line had to be built so that the train first goes forwards, then backwards to another track which leads upwards off the previous one, and this manoeuvre is repeated several times until it gets to the top and starts its descent along a stream which eventually leads into the Vilcanota. On the train we met a couple of Chilean quacks who were selling herbs and telling fortunes. They were very friendly and shared the food they had in return for the maté we offered them. When we reached the ruins, we came across a group playing football and got ourselves invited to play. After a couple of flashy tackles I admitted in all humility to having played first division football in Buenos Aires with Alberto, who showed off his skill in midfield on a pitch which the locals call a pampa. Our relatively brilliant performance got us noticed by the owner of the ball who also turned out to be manager of the hotel. He invited us to spend a couple of days there until his next load of Americans arrived in their special railcar. As well as being a fine person, Señor Soto was very knowledgeable, and after we'd exhausted the topic of sport which was his passion, he told us a lot about Inca culture.

We were very sorry when it was time to go. We had a last exquisite coffee made by Señora Soto before boarding the little train for its twelve-hour journey back to Cuzco. This kind of train has a third-class carriage for the local indians: they're like the ones used to transport cattle in Argentina, except that the smell of cow dung is much more pleasant than its human equivalent. The somewhat primitive idea the indians have of modesty and hygiene means that, regardless of sex or age, they do their business by the side of the road, the women wiping themselves with their skirts, the men not at all, and carry on as before. The petticoats of indian women with children are veritable warehouses of excrement, since they wipe the kids with them whenever they have a bowel movement. The tourists travelling in their comfortable railcars can only have the very vaguest idea of how the indians live, gleaned from a quick glance as they whizz by our train which has to stop to let them past. The fact that it was the North American archaeologist Bingham who discovered the ruins and published his findings in anecdotal articles easily accessible to the general public, has meant that Machu Picchu is very famous in the US and most North Americans visiting Peru come here (they usually fly direct to Lima, tour Cuzco, visit the ruins and go straight home, without bothering to see anything else).

The archaeological museum in Cuzco is not very good. By the time the authorities realized the amount of treasure being smuggled out, it was too late. Treasure hunters, tourists, foreign archaeologists, in fact anyone with any interest in the subject at all, had systematically looted the area and what ended up in the museum was what was left, little more than the dregs. Nevertheless, for people like us who didn't know much about archaeology and had only vague and recently gleaned notions of Inca civilization, there was enough to see and we spent several days in it. The curator was a very knowledgeable mestizo with a passionate interest in the race whose blood ran through his veins. He spoke of past glories and present poverty, of the pressing need to educate the indians, as a first step towards their complete rehabilitation. He insisted that improving the standard of living of indian families as quickly as possible was the only way to mitigate the soporific effect of coca and alcohol and talked of spreading a real knowledge of the Quechua nation so that the people of that race could feel proud of their past rather than, looking at their present, ashamed of being indian or mestizo. The coca problem was being debated in the UN at the time and we told him about our unfortunate experience with it. He said the same had happened to him and started cursing those who make a quick profit from poisoning large numbers of people. Together the Collas and Quechuas form the majority in Peru, and they are the ones who consume coca. The curator's half-indian features and his eyes shining with enthusiasm and faith in the future were another of the museum's treasures, but his was a living museum, proof of a race still fighting for its own identity.

HUAMBO

Having run out of doorbells to ring, we followed Gardel's advice and turned northward.[28] We were forced to stop in Abancay because that was where the lorries left for Huancar-ama, the town near the leper colony at Huambo. Our method of cadging bed and board (Civil Guard and hospital) didn't change, nor did the one for hitching a lift, except that we had to wait two days for the latter because it was Holy Week and there were very few lorries. We wandered round the little town without finding anything interesting enough to take our minds off our hunger, the hospital food being very meagre. Lying in the grass by the stream, we watched the changing evening sky, dreaming of past loves, or seeing in each cloud a more tempt-ing version of ordinary food.

On our way back to the police station to sleep, we took a short cut and got completely lost. After crossing fields and walls, we eventually landed up in the patio of a house. We'd climbed the stone wall when we saw a dog and his master looking like phantoms in the full moon. What we didn't reckon on was that we, silhouetted against the light, must have looked much more terrifying. Anyway, the response to my polite 'Good evening' was unintelligible sounds in which I thought I caught the word 'Viracocha!'[29] before man and dog fled into the house ignoring our friendly greetings and apologies. We

---

[28] An allusion to a famous line by the Argentine actor and composer of tangos, Carlos Gardel.

[29] The Inca Creator-God. The term is sometimes also used by indians for white people.

left calmly by the front gate on to a path which looked like a proper right of way.

In a moment of boredom we went to the church to watch a local ceremony. The poor priest was trying to produce the three-hour sermon but by then – about ninety minutes into it – he had run out of platitudes. He gazed at his congregation with imploring eyes while he waved a shaking hand at some spot in the church. 'Look, look, the Lord hath come, the Lord is with us, His spirit is guiding us.' After a moment's pause, the priest set off on his load of nonsense again and, just when he seemed about to dry up again, in a moment of high drama, he launched into a similar phrase. The fifth or sixth time poor Christ was announced, we got a fit of giggles and left in a hurry.

I don't know what brought on the attack (though I bet one of the faithful does), but by the time we got to Huancarama I could hardly stand up. I didn't have any adrenalin and my asthma was getting worse. Wrapped in a police blanket, I watched the rain and chain-smoked, the black tobacco helping to relieve my fatigue. It wasn't until dawn that I managed to fall asleep leaning against a post on the veranda. By morning I was a bit better and some adrenalin Alberto had found, plus several aspirins, left me feeling like new again.

We introduced ourselves to the lieutenant governor, a sort of village mayor, to beg a couple of horses to take us to the leper colony. He gave us a warm welcome and promised us two horses at the police station in five minutes. While we were waiting, we watched a ragged group of lads being put through their paces on the shouted orders of the soldier who had been so kind to us the day before. When he saw us, he saluted with the greatest respect, then carried on barking instructions for all kinds of drills to the squaddies in his charge. In Peru, only one in five young men of eligible age actually does military service, but the rest do lots of drills every Sunday and these were the current victims. In fact, they were all victims: the conscripts had to put up with their instructor's anger and he with his pupils' lethargy. Not understanding Spanish or why they had to turn one way or the other and march and halt just because the officer said so, they did it all with bad grace and were enough to make anyone lose their temper.

The horses arrived and the soldier gave us a guide who only spoke Quechua. We set off up a mountain track which to any other horse would have been impossible, led by the guide on foot who held our bridles over the tricky parts. We'd gone about two-thirds of the way when an old woman and a boy appeared. They grabbed our reins and launched into a tirade of which we only understood a word something like 'horse'. At first we thought they were selling wicker baskets, because the old woman was carrying lots of them. 'Me not want buy, me not want,' I kept telling her, and would have continued in the same vein, if Alberto had not reminded me we were talking to Quechuas, not relatives of Tarzan and the Apes. We finally met someone coming in the opposite direction who spoke Spanish and explained that these indians owned our horses; they'd been riding past the lieutenant governor's house when he had commandeered their horses for us. My horse belonged to one of the conscripts, who had come seven leagues to comply with his military duty, and the poor old woman lived in the opposite direction to the way we were going. What could we decently do but hand over the horses and continue on foot? The guide went on ahead, carrying our worldly goods on his back. So we walked the last league to the leper colony where we gave our guide one *sol* for his trouble, for which he thanked us profusely though it was only a pittance.

We were received by the head of the clinic, Señor Montejo. He said he couldn't put us up but would send us to a nearby landowner's house, which is what he did. The rancher gave us a room with beds and food, just what we needed. The next morning we went to visit the patients in the little hospital. The people running it do an unsung but praiseworthy job. The general conditions are appalling; thirty-one hopeless cases spend their lives in an area smaller than half a block, two thirds of which is the sick zone. They wait for death with indifference (at least I think they do). Sanitary conditions are terrible, and though this might not bother the indians from the mountains, people from a different background, even those only slightly more educated, find this very unpleasant. The thought of having to spend their lives between these four adobe walls, surrounded by people who speak another language and four orderlies whom they see for only a short time every day, causes mental breakdown.

We went into a room with a straw roof, slatted ceiling and earth floor. A fair-skinned girl was reading *Cousin Basilio* by Queirós. As we talked, the girl began weeping disconsolately and said this life was a calvary. The poor girl was from the Amazon area and had gone to Cuzco where they diagnosed the disease and said they would send her somewhere much better to be cured. While the hospital in Cuzco was by no means brilliant, it did have a certain amount of comfort. I think the word 'calvary' to describe this girl's case was absolutely right. The only decent thing in the hospital was the drug treatment, the rest was bearable only to the fatalist, resigned nature of Peruvian mountain indians. The stupidity of the local people only made things worse for both patients and medical staff. One of them told us that the surgeon at the clinic needed to perform an operation too serious to do on a kitchen table without surgical equipment. When he asked for a place in a nearby hospital at Andahuaylas, in the morgue if need be, the answer was no, so the patient received no treatment and died.

Señor Montejo told us that when the leper colony was founded, thanks to the efforts of the eminent leprologist Dr Pesce, he himself had been responsible for organizing the new services from the start. When he arrived in Huancarama, none of the hotels would give him a room for the night, the few friends he had in town refused to put him up and since it was raining he had been forced to spend the night in a pigsty. The patient I mentioned earlier had to walk to the leper colony because no one would lend her and her companion horses, and this was years after the colony had been founded.

After a warm welcome, we were taken to see a new hospital being built a few kilometres from the old one. The orderlies' eyes shone with pride when they asked us what we thought of it, as if they had built it brick by adobe brick with their own hands, so it seemed churlish to criticize. But the new leper colony has the same disadvantages as the old: it has no laboratory or surgical facilities and, to make matters worse, it is in an area infected by mosquitoes, real torture for anyone forced to spend all day there. Of course, it has room for 250 patients, a resident doctor and better sanitary conditions, but there's still a lot of room for improvement.

After two days in the area my asthma was getting worse, so we decided to leave and get some proper treatment.

On horses provided by the rancher who had lodged us, we set off back to town, still with the same laconic Quechua-speaking guide who the landowner insisted should carry our bags. For rich people in this area it's perfectly natural for a servant to carry anything heavy and put up with any discomfort, even if he's the one on foot. We waited till we were out of sight round the first bend and took our bags from our guide, but there was no sign on his enigmatic face to show whether he appreciated our gesture or not.

Back in Huancarama, we stayed at the Civil Guard post again until we found a lorry going further north. We were lucky the next day. After an exhausting journey, we finally reached the town of Andahuaylas, where I went to the hospital to recuperate.

STILL HEADING NORTH

A FTER two days in the hospital and at least partially recovered, we appealed once again to the charity of our great friends the Civil Guard, who received us with their usual good will. We had so little money we hardly dared eat, but we didn't want to get jobs until we reached Lima because we'd a reasonable chance of better paid work there, so we could save enough to continue our journey, since there was still no mention of turning back.

The first night of waiting was quite agreeable because the lieutenant in charge of the post, an obliging fellow, invited us to eat with him and we were able to store up for whatever lay ahead. The next two days, however, were marked only by hunger, now our constant companion, and boredom; we couldn't go very far from the post since that was where the lorry drivers had to get their papers checked before starting or continuing their journeys.

At the end of the third day, our fifth in Andahuaylas, we finally found a lorry going to Ayacucho. Not before time, in fact, because Alberto had got angry when he saw one of the guards insulting an indian woman who had come to bring food to her husband in the jail. His reaction must have seemed very odd to people who considered indians as objects, allowed to stay alive but no more, so we were out of favour after that.

At nightfall we left the town where circumstance had kept us prisoner for several days. The lorry had to climb to cross the mountains blocking the northern access to Andahuaylas and the temperature dropped by the minute. To cap it all, we were soaked by one of those violent rainstorms typical of this part of the world and we had no defence against it, stuck as we were in the back of a lorry taking ten bullocks to Lima and expected to keep an eye on them, along with an indian lad who acted as driver's assistant. We spent the night in a village called Chincheros. We were so cold we forgot we were penniless pariahs and ate a modest meal and asked for one bed between two, all accompanied, needless to say, by tears and tales of woe that had some effect on the owner at least: he let us have the lot for five *soles*. The next day we continued on our way, passing from deep ravines to what they call 'pampas', the flat plateaux on the tops of the mountain chains throughout Peru; there are no plains at all in the country's irregular topography apart from the forested areas in the Amazon. Our job got more difficult as the hours went by, since the layer of sawdust the bullocks were standing on disappeared and, tired from standing in the same position hour after hour, absorbing all the lorry's jolts, they started falling over. We had to get them back on their feet because if any got trampled, they might die.

At one point Alberto thought one animal's horn was hurting another's eye and told the indian lad who was near it. With a shrug of his shoulders which expressed the whole spirit of his race, he said, 'Why bother, all it'll ever see is shit,' and calmly went back to the knot he'd been tying when interrupted.

We finally reached Ayacucho, famous in the history of the Americas for the decisive battle Bolívar won on the plains outside the town. The inadequate street lighting which plagues all Peruvian mountain towns seemed at its worst there; the electric lights gave off only the most feeble of orange glows in the night. A gentleman whose hobby was collecting foreign friends invited us to sleep at his house and got us a lift the next day in a lorry going north, so we only visited one or two of the thirty-three churches the little town boasts. We said goodbye to our new friend and set off again for Lima.

THROUGH CENTRAL PERU

O UR JOURNEY continued much the same, with us eating now and again when some charitable soul took pity on our poverty. Even so, we never ate much and things got worse when that evening we were told there was a landslide up ahead and we would have to spend the night in a village called Anco. We set off again early, back in our lorry, but not far up the road we reached the landslide and had to spend the day there, famished yet curious, watching the workmen dynamite the huge boulders which had fallen across the road. For every labourer, there were at least five officious foremen, shouting their mouths off and hindering the others, who were not exactly a hive of industry either.

We tried to stave off our hunger by going down for a swim in the river, but the water was too icy to stay in for long and you might say neither of us stands the cold very well. In the end, after another of our sob stories, one man gave us some corn on the cob and another a cow's heart and some innards. A lady lent us a pot but just as we'd begun making our meal, the workmen cleared the road and the line of lorries began to move. The lady reclaimed her pot and we had to eat the corn raw and keep the uncooked meat. To add to our misery, a terrible rainstorm turned the road into a dangerous mudbath and it was nearly dark. The lorries on the far side of the avalanche came through first because there was only room for one at a time, then it was our turn. We were near the head of a long queue, but the differential on the first lorry broke when the tractor helping the manoeuvre pushed too hard, and we were all stuck again. Eventually, a jeep with a winch on the front came down the hill and heaved the lorry to the side of the road so we could all pass. The lorry drove through the night, and as usual we'd go from quite sheltered valleys on to those freezing Peruvian pampas where the icy wind cut straight through our sodden clothes. Alberto and I huddled together, our teeth chattering, taking turns to stretch out our legs to stop them getting cramp. By now, our hunger was a strange feeling no longer in one particular place but all over our bodies, making us edgy and bad tempered.

In Huancayo, where we arrived as dawn was breaking, we walked the fifteen blocks between where the lorry dropped us and the Civil Guard post, our usual stopover. We bought bread, made maté and were starting to unpack the famous heart and innards but hadn't even got the fire going when a lorry offered to take us to Oxapampa. Our interest in the place lay in the fact that the mother of a friend of ours in Argentina lived there, or so we thought. We were hoping she would assuage our hunger for a few days and perhaps offer us a *sol* or two. So we left Huancayo again without even seeing it, driven on by the call of our empty stomachs.

The first part of the journey, passing through several villages, was fine, but at six in the evening we began a dangerous descent down a road hardly wide enough for one vehicle at a time. Traffic was normally restricted to one way only each day, but this particular day was for some reason or other an exception, and lorries passing each other, with much yelling, manoeuvring and rear wheels hanging over the edge of seemingly bottomless precipices, was not exactly a reassuring sight. Alberto and I crouched, one at each corner of the lorry, ready to leap off if the need arose, but the indians travelling with us didn't move so much as an inch. Our fears were justified, however, since a fair number of crosses line this stretch of the mountainside, marking the exploits of less fortunate colleagues among the drivers. And every lorry that fell took its terrible human cargo two hundred metres down the abyss, where a fast-flowing torrent put paid to any tiny chance of survival. According to the locals, all those who've gone over the edge have been killed, with not a single injured survivor to tell the tale.

Luckily, on this occasion nothing untoward happened and we arrived at about ten at night in a village called La Merced. It was situated in a low-lying, tropical area and looked like a typical jungle village. Yet another charitable soul offered us a bed and a hefty meal. The food was included at the last moment when the man came to see if we were comfortable and we didn't have time to hide the peel of some oranges we had picked to calm our hunger pangs.

At the Civil Guard post we weren't very happy to learn that lorries didn't have to stop to be registered. That made it hard for us to hitch. While we were there, we heard two people reporting a murder; they were the victim's son and a volatile mulatto who claimed to be an intimate friend of the dead man. The whole thing had happened mysteriously some days earlier, and the prime suspect was an indian whose photo the two men had brought. The sergeant showed it to us, saying, 'Look, gentlemen, the classic example of a murderer.' We agreed enthusiastically, but when we got outside I asked Alberto, 'Who's the murderer?' And he thought the same as I did, that the mulatto looked more likely than the indian.

During the long hours waiting for our lift, we made friends with someone who said he could arrange everything at no cost to us. He did in fact talk to a lorry driver, who agreed to take us. After we'd climbed aboard, we found he had merely arranged for us to pay five *soles* less than the twenty the driver usually charged. When we pleaded that we were completely broke, which was very close to the truth, he promised to pay.

He was as good as his word, and, when we arrived, took us home for the night into the bargain. Although wider than the previous one, the road was still narrow, but it was pretty and wound through forest or tropical fruit plantations: bananas, papayas and others. It was up and down all the way to Oxapampa, which was a thousand metres above sea level, our destination and the end of the highway.

In the lorry with us was the mulatto who had reported the murder. During one of our stops he bought us a meal, lecturing us on coffee, papaya and black slaves in Peru, of whom his grandfather had been one. He said this quite openly but it was clear he was ashamed of it. In any case, Alberto and I agreed to exonerate him from any blame for the murder of his friend.

OUR HOPES ARE DASHED

To our disgust, we learned next morning that our friend in Buenos Aires had given us the wrong information and his mother had not lived in Oxapampa for quite some time. A brother-in-law did live there, though, and he had to take on our dead weight. The reception was magnificent and we had a slap-up meal, but we realized we were welcome only out of traditional Peruvian hospitality. We decided to ignore any-thing but direct marching orders, as we had absolutely no money and a legacy of several days' hunger, and could eat only in the home of our reluctant friends.

We had a wonderful day; swimming in the river, free of care, good food and lots of it, delicious coffee. But all good things come to an end and by the evening of the second day, the engineer – because our 'host' was an engineer – came up with a solution that was not only effective but cheap: a highways inspector had offered to take us all the way to Lima. We were delighted since the panorama looked bleak there and we wanted to get to the capital to try our luck, so we fell for it, hook, line and sinker.

That night we climbed into the back of a pick-up truck which, after a downpour which soaked us to the skin, left us at two in the morning in San Ramón, less than halfway to Lima. The driver told us to wait while he changed vehicles and left his assistant with us to allay any suspicions. Ten minutes later he too disappeared off to buy cigarettes, and this pair of Argentine wiseguys breakfasted at five in the morning on the bitter realization that we had been fooled all along the line. I hope the driver gets his come-uppance ... (I had a gut feeling about it, but he seemed such a nice guy that we believed everything ... even the change of vehicle.) Shortly before dawn, we came across a couple of drunks and did our brilliant 'anniversary' routine. It goes like this:

1. One of us says something in a loud voice immediately identifying us as Argentine, something with a *che* in it and other typical expressions and pronunciation. The victim asks where we're from and we strike up a conversation.

2. We begin our tale of woe but don't make too much of it, all the while staring into the distance.

3. Then I butt in and ask what the date is. Someone says it and Alberto sighs and says: 'What a coincidence, it was exactly

a year ago.' The victim asks what was a year ago, and we reply that was when we started out on our trip.

4. Alberto, who is much more brazen than me, then heaves a tremendous sigh and says, 'Shame we're in such dire straits, we won't be able to celebrate' (he says this as a kind of aside to me). The victim immediately offers to pay, we pretend to refuse for a while saying we can't possibly pay him back, etc., then finally we accept.

5. After the first drink, I adamantly refuse another and Alberto makes fun of me. Our host gets annoyed and insists, I keep refusing but I won't say why. The victim keeps asking until I confess, rather shamefacedly, that in Argentina it's the custom to eat when we drink. Just how much we eat depends on what we think we can get away with, but the technique never fails.

We tried it again in San Ramón and as usual we helped down an enormous amount of drink with something more solid. All morning we lay by the riverbank, a lovely spot, but our aesthetic perception of it was hampered by terrifying visions of all kinds of delicious food. Near by, the tempting roundness of oranges poked over a fence. Our feast was fierce but sad, however, because one minute our stomachs felt full and acidy and the next we had pangs of gnawing hunger again.

We were so famished we decided to shake off any vestiges of shame and head straight for the local hospital. This time it was Alberto who was strangely embarrassed and it was up to me to intone the following diplomatically worded speech:

'Doctor' (we found one in the hospital), 'I'm a medical student, my friend is a biochemist. We are both Argentine and we're hungry. We want to eat.' The poor doctor was so astonished by this frontal attack that he bought us a meal in the restaurant where he usually ate. We were brazen.

Without even thanking him because Alberto felt ashamed, we set about finding another lorry, which we eventually did. We were now on our way to Lima, comfortably installed in the driver's cab. He even bought us coffees from time to time.

We were climbing the narrow mountain road which had so terrified us on the way in and the driver was cheerfully telling us the history of every roadside cross we passed, when all of a sudden he hit an enormous pothole in the middle of the road which any fool could have seen. We began to think he didn't know how to drive at all, but simple logic told us this could not be true, because on this road anyone but an experienced driver would have gone over the edge long ago. With tact and patience, Alberto slowly dragged the truth out of him. The man had had an accident which, according to him, had affected his eyesight, which was why he hit potholes. We tried to make him see how dangerous it was, not only for him but also for the people with him. The driver was adamant: it was his job, he was very well paid by a boss who never asked *how* he got to places, only *if* he got there. Besides, his driving licence had cost a lot of money because of the big bribe he'd had to pay for it.

The owner of the lorry got on further down the road. He was willing to take us to Lima but I, who was up top, had to hide when we came to police checkpoints because they weren't allowed to take passengers on goods vehicles like this one. The owner turned out to be a good bloke too and bought us food all the way to Lima. Before that, however, we went through La

Oroya, a mining town we would have liked to visit but couldn't because we didn't stop. La Oroya is about four thousand metres above sea level, and you can tell how harsh life is in the mine just from looking at it. Its tall chimneys belched out black smoke which covered everything in soot, and the faces of the miners in the streets were also impregnated with that age-old sadness of smoke which covers everything in a unifying monotonous grey, a perfect accompaniment to the grey mountain days. While it was still light, we crossed the highest point on the road, at 4,853 metres above sea level. The cold was intense even in the daytime. Wrapped in my travelling blanket, I stared out at the landscape on all sides, reciting all kinds of verses, lulled by the roar of the lorry engine.

That night we slept just outside the city, and early the next day we were in Lima.

CITY OF THE VICEROYS

W E HAD reached the end of one of the most important stages of our journey, we hadn't a cent and practically no chance of making any money in the short term, but we were happy.

Lima is an attractive city which has already buried its colonial past (at least compared to Cuzco) behind new houses. Its reputation as a beautiful city is not justified, but it has very nice residential suburbs, broad avenues and exceedingly pleasant resorts along the coast. Wide roads take the inhabitants of Lima to the port of Callao in just a few minutes. The port is not especially interesting (all ports seem built to a standard design) except for the fort, the scene of many battles. Standing beside the enormous walls we marvelled at Lord Cochrane's feat when, at the head of his South American sailors, he attacked and took this bastion of resistance in one of the most glorious episodes in the history of the liberation of South America.

The most memorable part of Lima is the centre of the city around its magnificent cathedral, so different from the monolithic mass of Cuzco, where the *conquistadores* crudely celebrated their own grandeur. In Lima, on the other hand, the art is more stylized, you might almost say effeminate: its towers are tall and slender, perhaps the most slender of all the cathedral towers in the Spanish colonies. The most sumptuous work is not in wood carving as in Cuzco, but in gold. The naves are light and airy, compared to the dark, hostile caverns of the Inca capital. The paintings are also light, almost cheery, done by schools which came after the hermetic mestizos who painted their saints with a dark, fettered rage. The church façades and altars demonstrate the complete range of Churrigueresque art in their love of gold. It was because of this vast wealth that the aristocracy resisted the armies of America up to the very last. Lima is the perfect example of a Peru which has never emerged from its feudal, colonial state. It is still waiting for the blood of a truly liberating revolution.

But the corner of this aristocratic city we liked best, and where we often went to relive our impressions of Machu Picchu, was the Archaeological and Anthropological Museum. Created by a scholar of pure indian blood, Don Julio Tello, it contains extraordinarily valuable collections, reflecting whole cultures.

119

It is not all that similar to Córdoba, but it has that same look of a colonial, or rather provincial, city. We went to the consulate to get our letters and, after reading them, went to try our luck with an introduction we had for a penpusher at the Foreign Office who, needless to say, gave us short shrift. We went from one police station to another – in one we even got a plate of rice – and in the afternoon we went to see Dr Hugo Pesce, the expert in leprology, who was amazingly friendly for someone so famous. He got us beds in a leper hospital and invited us to dinner that night. He turned out to be fascinating to talk to. We left very late.

We also got up late and had breakfast. Nobody had been told to feed us so we decided to walk down to Callao and visit the port. It was hard work because being 1 May there was no public transport and we had to do the whole fourteen kilometres on foot. There is nothing special to see in Callao. There weren't even any Argentine boats. Cheekier than ever, we scrounged a bit of food at a barracks and then hoofed it back to Lima where we ate at Dr Pesce's house again. He told us stories about different types of leprosy.

The next morning we went to the Archaeological and Anthropological Museum. Magnificent, but we didn't have time to see the whole of it. In the afternoon we were given a guided tour of the leper hospital[30] by Dr Molina who, apart from being a leprologist, is apparently a magnificent thoracic surgeon. Then it was off to dinner at Dr Pesce's again.

[30] The Hospital de Guía.

The whole of Saturday morning was wasted in the centre trying to change fifty Swedish *krone*; we finally managed after a lot of hassle. Then we spent the afternoon in the laboratory, which wasn't much to write home about, in fact it left a lot to be desired. The bibliographic records, on the other hand, were excellent, clearly and methodically organized and very comprehensive. Dr Pesce's for dinner, of course, and we had the usual really animated chat.

Sunday was a big day for us. It was our first time at a bullfight and although it was what they call a *novillada*, that is, poor quality bulls and toreadors, we were very excited; so much so that I had trouble concentrating on one of Tello's books I was reading that morning in the library. We arrived just as the bullfight was starting and as we went in a novice toreador was killing the bull, but not by the usual *coup de grâce* method. The result was that the bull lay on the ground in agony for about ten minutes while the toreador tried to finish it off and the public booed. The third bull produced considerable excitement when it spectacularly gored the toreador and tossed him in the air, but that was all. The fiesta ended with the inglorious death of the sixth bull. I don't see any art in it. Courage, to a certain extent; skill, not much; excitement, relative. All in all, it depends what there is to do on a Sunday.

On Monday morning we went to the museum again, then to Dr Pesce's house in the evening. That night we met a Dr Valenza, a professor of psychiatry, another good talker who told us war stories and other anecdotes: 'The other day I went to our local cinema to see a film with Cantinflas. Everyone was laughing but I didn't understand a thing. I wasn't alone though, no one else understood anything either. So, why do they laugh? They're really laughing at themselves, they were all laughing at a part of themselves. We're a young country, with no tradition, no education, barely discovered. So they were laughing at all the defects of our infant civilization . . . But has North America grown up, despite its skyscrapers, its cars, its luxuries? Has it matured? No, the differences are superficial, not fundamental, all America is alike in this. Watching Cantinflas, I understood Panamericanism!'

Tuesday was no different in terms of museums, but at three in the afternoon we went to see Dr Pesce and he gave Alberto a white suit and me a jacket of the same colour. Everyone agrees we look almost human. The rest of the day wasn't important.

Several days have passed and we are raring to be off, but we still don't know exactly when we're leaving. We should have left two days ago, but the lorry taking us is still here. The various aspects of our journey are all going well. As far as extending our knowledge is concerned, we've been to museums and libraries. The only really useful one is Dr Tello's Archaeological and Anthropological Museum. From the scientific point of view, leprosy that is, we have met Dr Pesce; the others are just disciples of his and are a long way off producing anything of note. There are no biochemists in Peru, so specialist doctors do the laboratory work and Alberto talked to some of them to give them contacts in Buenos Aires. He got on well with two of them but the third . . . The trouble was that Alberto introduced himself as Dr Granado, leprosy specialist, etc., and they took him for a medical doctor. So this twit he was talking to came out with: 'No, we don't have biochemists here. There's a law prohibiting doctors from opening chemists' shops, so we don't let pharmacists meddle in things they don't understand.' Alberto was ready to explode so I nudged him in the ribs and he calmed down.

Although it was very simple, one of the things which affected us most in Lima was the send-off we got from the hospital patients. They collected 100.50 *soles*, which they presented to us with a very grandiloquent letter. Afterwards some of them came up personally and some had tears in their eyes as they thanked us for coming, spending time with them, accepting their presents, sitting listening to football on the radio with them. If anything were to make us seriously specialize in leprosy, it would be the affection the patients show us wherever we go.

As a city, Lima doesn't live up to its long tradition as a viceregal seat, but its residential suburbs are attractive and its new streets nice and wide too. One interesting detail was the police presence surrounding the Colombian embassy. No less than fifty policemen, uniformed and plainclothed, do permanent guard duty round the whole block.

The first day of our journey out of Lima was uneventful. We saw the road to La Oroya but the rest we did during the night, arriving at Cerro de Pasco at dawn. We travelled with the Becerra brothers, called Cambalache, Camba for short. They were good blokes, especially the eldest one. We drove the whole day, descending into warmer climes, and the headache and general nausea I'd had since Ticlio, at 4,853 metres the highest point above sea level, started to subside. Just past Huánuco and nearing Tingo María, the front left axle broke but luckily the wheel got stuck in the mudguard so we didn't turn over. We had to spend the night there and I wanted to give myself an injection but as luck would have it the syringe broke.

The next day went by boringly and asthmatically, but that evening took a fortunate turn for Alberto and me when he mentioned in a melancholy voice that we'd been on the road for exactly six months. That was the signal for the *pisco* to flow. By the third bottle, Alberto tottered to his feet and abandoning a little monkey he was holding disappeared from the scene. Camba junior carried on for another half bottle, and collapsed right there.

The next morning we left in a hurry, before the owner was awake, because we hadn't paid the bill and the Cambas were short of money because of the axle. We drove the whole day until we finally had to stop at one of those road-closed barriers the army puts up when it rains.

Off again the next day and another halt at a barrier. They didn't let the caravan move on until the late afternoon and it was stopped again at a town called Nescuilla, our target for the day.

The road was still closed the next day, so we went to the army post to ask for grub. We set off in the afternoon, taking with us a wounded soldier, which would get us through the army road blocks. And in fact, a few kilometres further on, when other lorries were being stopped, we were allowed through to Pucallpa where we arrived after dark. Camba junior bought us a meal and as a goodbye we drank four bottles of wine which made him all sentimental and he swore eternal love. He then paid for a hotel room for us.

The main problem now was getting to Iquitos; so we buckled down to the task. Our first target was the mayor, a certain

Cohen, who we were told was Jewish but a good sort; there was no doubt he was Jewish, the problem was finding out if he was a good sort. He palmed us off on the shipping agents, who then palmed us off on the captain, who received us well enough and promised, as a huge concession, to charge us a third-class fare and let us travel first class. Not happy with this, we went to see the commander of the garrison who said he could do nothing for us. Then his deputy, after a hideous interrogation in which he showed how stupid he was, promised to help.

That afternoon we went swimming in the River Ucayali which looks rather like the Upper Paraná. We came across the deputy who said he'd got a really interesting deal for us: as a special favour to him, the captain had agreed to charge us a third-class fare and put us in first class, big deal.

In the place where we were swimming, there were a pair of strangely shaped fish which the locals call *bufeo*. The story goes that they eat men, rape women and thousands of weird things like that. It is apparently a river dolphin which has, among other strange characteristics, genitals like a woman's, so the indians use it as a substitute, but they have to kill the animal when they've finished coitus because a contraction in the genital area stops the penis coming out. In the evening we tackled the always dismal task of asking our colleagues at the hospital for lodging. The welcome was, naturally, frosty, and we would have been shown the door had our passivity not won the day and we got two beds on which to lay our weary bones.

DOWN THE UCAYALI

PACKS on our backs, looking like explorers, we boarded *La Cenepa* just before it left. As promised, the captain put us in first class where we mixed with the privileged passengers. After a few warning blasts, the boat pulled away from the shore and we began the second stage of our journey to San Pablo. When the houses in Pucallpa were out of sight and the view was of uninterrupted jungle vegetation, people left the rails and gathered around the gambling tables. We were nervous about playing but Alberto was inspired and won ninety *soles* at a card game called 21, something like our $7\frac{1}{2}$. This win didn't make him very popular with the other gamblers on board, because he had played with an initial stake of just one *sol*.

There wasn't much opportunity to make the acquaintance of the other passengers on that first day and we kept to ourselves, not joining in the general conversation. The food was bad and there wasn't much of it. The boat didn't sail at night because the river was too low. There were very few mosquitoes, and although we were told this was unusual we didn't believe it, because by now we were used to the way people exaggerate when trying to describe difficult situations.

Early next morning, we set sail again. The day passed uneventfully, apart from making friends with a girl who was a bit of a tart and probably thought we had a few *pesos* despite the anguished tears we shed whenever money was mentioned. In the late afternoon, when the boat pulled in to moor by the riverbank, the mosquitoes were bent on proving they really did exist; swarms of them attacked during the night. Wrapped in his sleeping bag and with a net over his face, Alberto managed to get some sleep, but I felt an asthma attack coming on, so what with that and the mosquitoes, I didn't close my eyes till morning. My memory of that night has dimmed, but I can still feel the skin on my buttocks grown to mammoth proportions from so many bites.

The whole of the next day I spent dozing in some corner or other, snatching winks of sleep in borrowed hammocks. The asthma didn't look like abating so I had to take drastic measures and get an anti-asthmatic by the prosaic method of paying for it. It helped calm the attack. We stared dreamily out at the tempting jungle beyond the riverbank, with its mysterious greenery. My asthma and the mosquitoes clipped my wings somewhat, but virgin forests have such a fascination for spirits like ours that physical problems and all the forces nature could unleash only served to increase my desire.

The days passed monotonously. The only entertainment was gambling, which we couldn't enjoy fully because of our economic plight. Two days went by uneventfully. Normally this trip takes four days but with the river so low we had to stop every night; this not only prolonged the journey but turned us into sacrificial victims for the mosquitoes. The food is better in first class and there are fewer mosquitoes, but I'm not sure we got the best of the bargain. We get on much better with simple sailors than with that middle class which, rich or not, is too attached to the memory of what it once was to pay any attention to two penniless travellers. They are as ignorant as the next man, but their petty victory in life has gone to their heads, and the banal opinions they utter come with the arrogance of being proffered by them. My asthma got worse, even though I was following my diet to the letter.

A light caress from the little tart who was commiserating with my sorry physical state pricked the dormant memories of my pre-adventurer life. That night as the mosquitoes kept me awake, I thought of Chichina, now a distant dream, a very enjoyable dream which ended, unusually for this kind of notion, with more honey in my memory than gall. I sent her a gentle, serene kiss, that of an old friend who knows and understands her; then my mind wandered on to Malagueño, in whose hall late at night she was probably whispering those strange intricate phrases of hers to some new suitor at that very moment. The immense dome of the starry sky above me twinkled merrily, as if saying yes to the question which rose from deep inside me: 'Is this worth it?'

Two more days: nothing new. The confluence of the Ucayali and the Marañon, the origin of the earth's mightiest river, has nothing earth shattering about it: it is simply two masses of muddy water which meet to form one – slightly wider, probably deeper, but nothing more. I have no adrenalin left and my asthma is getting worse and worse; I eat little more than a handful of rice and drink maté. The last day, when we were almost there, we ran into a fierce storm and the boat had to stop. The mosquitoes swarmed over us, worse than ever, as if taking revenge for the fact we would soon be out of their range. The night seemed endless, filled with desperate slaps and impatient shrieks, continual card games to numb our senses and haphazard phrases tossed out to keep some kind of conversation going and make the time pass more quickly. The next morning, a hammock hangs empty in the rush to disembark and I lie down. As if bewitched, I feel as though a coiled spring is unwinding inside me, sending me spiralling into the heavens, or down into the abyss, who knows which . . . A rough shake from Alberto wakes me up. ' "Pelao", we're here.' The river had broadened out to reveal in front of us a flat low town with a few taller buildings, encircled by jungle and coloured by the red earth.

Sunday, the day of our arrival in Iquitos. We tied up at the quay early and went straight to talk to the head of the International Co-operation Service, since the man we had an introduction to, Dr Chávez Pastor, was not in Iquitos. Anyway, they treated us well, put us up in the yellow fever section and gave us food at the hospital. I still had asthma and couldn't shake off my wretched bellows-like wheezing, even with as many as four adrenalin shots a day.

I was no better the next day and I spent it on my bed, or rather 'adrenalizing myself'.

The following day I made up my mind to follow a strict morning diet and a relatively strict one at night, cutting out rice. I got a bit better, but not much. That night, we saw *Stromboli* with Ingrid Bergman, directed by Rossellini. The only rating you can give it is bad.

Wednesday was an important date for us; we learned we would be leaving the next day. This cheered us up no end since my asthma had immobilized me and we spent the days lying in bed.

The next day we got ourselves psychologically fired up for leaving. But the day passed and we still hadn't weighed anchor, and departure was set for the following afternoon.

Certain that the owners' inertia could have us leaving later but never earlier, we slept late, had a stroll, then went to the library, where the assistant, in a flap, rushed in because *El Cisne* was sailing at 11.30 a.m. and it was already 11.05. We quickly got our stuff together and, because of my asthma, took a taxi which charged us half a Peruvian pound for eight blocks of Iquitos. When we reached the boat it wasn't leaving until three, but we had to be on board at one. We daren't disobey and go for lunch at the hospital and besides it suited us not to, since this way we could 'forget' the syringe they had lent us. We ate badly and expensively with an indian from the Yagua tribe, strangely decked out in a red straw skirt and necklaces of the same straw; his name was Benjamín but he didn't speak much Spanish. He had a scar just above the shoulder blade, from a bullet shot at almost point-blank range, out of *'vinganza'* he said in a mixture of Spanish and Portuguese.

That night hordes of mosquitoes fought over our virgin flesh. There was a psychologically important moment on the trip when we learned you could get from Manaus to Venezuela by river. The day passed peacefully, and we had a good doze to catch up on sleep lost to the mosquitoes. That night, at about one, I was woken just as I'd got to sleep and told we had arrived in San Pablo. They advised Dr Bresciani, the medical director of the colony, who received us warmly and gave us a room for the night.

LETTER FROM ERNESTO TO HIS FATHER:
IQUITOS, 4 JUNE 1952

T HE BANKS of the great rivers are completely settled. To find savage tribes you have to follow the tributaries deep into the interior – a journey which, this time at least, we don't intend to make. Infectious diseases have disappeared, but we've nevertheless been vaccinated against typhoid and yellow fever and have a good supply of atebrine and quinine.

There are lots of diseases due to metabolic disorders caused by nutritional deficiencies in the food available in the jungle, but serious cases result only from going without vitamins for a week, and that's the longest time we'd be without proper food if we went by river. We're still not sure about this as we've been looking into the possibility of taking a plane to Bogotá, or at least Leguisamo, from where the roads are good. This isn't because we think the journey might be dangerous, but to save money, which might be important for me later on.

Away from scientific centres where we might be cut down to size, our journey becomes something of an event for the staff of the anti-leprosy hospitals and they treat us with a respect worthy of two visiting researchers. I've got really keen on leprology but I don't know how long for. The farewell which the patients in the Lima hospital gave us was enough to encourage us to carry on; they gave us a primus stove and collected a hundred *soles*, which in their economic circumstances is a fortune, and several of them said goodbye with tears in their eyes. Their appreciation stemmed from the fact that we didn't wear overalls or gloves, that we shook hands with them as we would with the next man, sat with them, chatting about this and that, and played football with them. This may seem pointless bravado, but the psychological benefit to these poor people – usually treated like animals – of being treated as normal human beings is incalculable and the risk incredibly remote. Until now the only staff to have been infected are a medical orderly in Indochina who lived with his patients, and a zealous monk whom I wouldn't like to vouch for.

THE SAN PABLO LEPER COLONY

THE NEXT day, Sunday, found us up and ready for a tour of the colony but, since it meant taking a boat upriver and it wasn't a working day, we couldn't. Instead we visited the nun who administered the colony, the masculine looking Mother Sor Alberto, then had a game of football in which we played very badly. My asthma began to subside.

On Monday, after sending some of our clothes to be washed, we went to visit the patients' compound. Six hundred of them live in typical jungle huts, quite independently, doing whatever they wish, working at their own jobs, in an organization which has taken on characteristics and a pace all its own. There is a local official, a judge, a policeman, etc. Dr Bresciani commands considerable respect and he clearly co-ordinates the whole colony, both protecting and bridging differences for groups which fight amongst themselves.

We visited the compound again on Tuesday, accompanying Dr Bresciani on his rounds as he examined the patients' nervous systems. He is working on a detailed study of nervous forms of leprosy based on four hundred cases. It will be a very interesting survey because most of the cases of leprosy in this region attack the nervous system. In fact, I didn't see a single patient without these symptoms. According to Dr Bresciani, Dr Souza Lima was interested in early nervous signs in the children living in the colony.

We visited the part of the colony reserved for the seventy or so healthy people. It lacks basic amenities, like all-day electric light, a refrigerator and a laboratory, but these are apparently being installed over the course of this year. They could do with a good microscope, a microtome, a laboratory technician – at the moment this post is occupied by Mother Margarita who is very nice but not very expert – and they need a surgeon to operate on nerves, eyes, etc. It is worth noting that, despite the enormous nervous problems, very few people are blind, which may perhaps help to demonstrate that the [. . .] has something to do with it, since most have had no treatment at all.

On Wednesday we did the rounds again, with a bit of fishing and swimming in between. At night I play chess with Dr Bresciani or we chat. The dentist, Dr Alfaro, is a wonderfully easygoing and friendly man.

Thursday is the colony's day off so we didn't go to the compound. We played football in the afternoon and I wasn't quite so bad in goal. In the morning we had tried to fish, fruitlessly.

On Friday I went back to the compound while Alberto stayed to do bacilloscopes with the cute nun, Mother Margarita. I caught two types of *sumbi* fish, called *mota*, one of which I gave to Dr Montoya.

SAINT GUEVARA'S DAY

O N SATURDAY 14 June 1952, I, a mere stripling, turned twenty-four, on the cusp of that transcendental quarter century, silver wedding of a life, which has not treated me too badly, all in all. In the morning early I went to the river to try my luck again with the fish, but fishing is like gambling: start by winning and you end up losing. In the afternoon we had a game of football, I in my usual place in goal, more successfully than on previous occasions. In the evening, after going to Dr Bresciani's house for a delicious feast, there was a party for us in the colony's dining room, with lots of the Peruvian national drink, *pisco*. Alberto is quite an expert on its effects on the central nervous system. When everyone was in high spirits, the colony's director proposed a very touching toast to us, and I, pretty '*pisco*-ed', produced something like the following:

'Well, it's my duty to reply to the toast proposed by Dr Bresciani with something more than the conventional gesture. In our present precarious state, all we have to offer are words and I would now like to use them to express my heartfelt thanks, and those of my friend, to the entire staff of the colony who, though they hardly know us, have demonstrated their affection so magnificently by celebrating my birthday as if it were one of your own. And I want to add something else. In a few days we'll be leaving Peru, so these words are also a farewell, and I'd like to stress my gratitude to all the people of this country, who over and over again since we arrived in Peru at Tacna have shown us the warmth of their hospitality. And I'd like to add another thought, nothing to do with this toast.

Although we're too insignificant to be spokesmen for such a noble cause, we believe, and this journey has only served to confirm this belief, that the division of America into unstable and illusory nations is a complete fiction. We are one single mestizo race with remarkable ethnographical similarities, from Mexico down to the Magellan Straits. And so, in an attempt to break free from all narrow-minded provincialism, I propose a toast to Peru and to a United America.'

My speech was received with loud applause. The party, which in these parts consists of downing as much alcohol as possible, went on until three in the morning, when we finally packed it in.

On Sunday morning we went to visit a tribe of Yaguas, the indians of the red straw. We walked for thirty minutes along a path which disproves rumours about deep dark jungle and reached a group of huts. It was interesting to see how they live outside under wooden planks and have a tiny hermetic straw hut to shelter in at night from the mosquitoes which attack in close formation. The women had given up traditional costumes for ordinary clothes so you can't admire their pairs of jugs.[31] The kids have big bellies and are rather skinny but the old people show no signs of the vitamin deficiency common among more developed people living in the jungle. Their main food is yucca, bananas, the fruit of the palm and animals they hunt with rifles. Their teeth are all rotten. They speak their own language, but understand Spanish, at least some do. In the afternoon we played football and I was a bit better but they put a sneaky goal past me. That night Alberto woke me with an

---

[31] In the original this is a pun: *'juego de té'*, i.e. tea (tits) set.

acute pain in his stomach, which turned out to be in the right iliac cavity; I was too tired to worry about someone else's aches and pains so I prescribed fortitude, turned over and slept till morning.

Monday is the day medicine is distributed in the compound. Alberto, well looked after by his beloved Mother Margarita, got penicillin religiously every four hours. Dr Bresciani told me he was expecting a raft with some animals on board, and we could take some clamps and planks to make a small raft of our own. We jumped at the idea and started making plans to go to Manaus, etc. I had an infected foot, so I sat out the afternoon game; instead I chatted with Dr Bresciani about everything under the sun and went to bed very late.

By Tuesday morning Alberto had recovered, so we went to the compound where Dr Montoya operated on the ulna in a leprous nervous system with apparently brilliant results, although the technique left a lot to be desired. In the afternoon, we went fishing in a nearby lagoon. We didn't catch anything of course, but on the way back I decided to swim across the Amazon which took me about two hours to the despair of Dr Montoya who didn't want to wait that long. There was a cosy party that night which ended in a serious fight with Señor Lezama Beltrán, an infantile introvert soul who was probably perverted as well. The poor man was drunk and furious because he wasn't invited to the party, so he started ranting and raving until someone gave him a black eye and a beating to boot. The incident rather upset us because the poor man, apart from being homosexual and a total bore, had been very nice to us and gave us each ten *soles*, making a grand total of: me 479, Alberto 163.50.

Wednesday was a rainy morning, so we didn't go to the compound and in fact it was a wasted day. I read some García Lorca, and later that night we watched the raft tie up at the jetty.

On Thursday morning, the medical staff's day off, we went with Dr Montoya to the other bank of the river to buy food. We went down a tributary of the Amazon, bought papayas, yucca, corn, fish, sugar cane, all very cheaply, and did a little fishing. Montoya caught a regular fish and I got a *mota*. On the way back, a strong wind whipped up the river and the captain, Roger Alvarez, was scared shitless seeing the waves swamp his canoe. I asked to take the helm but he wouldn't let me and we went to the bank to wait for the river to calm. We didn't get home until three in the afternoon. We had the fish cooked but that didn't fully satisfy our hunger. Roger gave us a shirt each and me a pair of trousers, so I increased my spiritual wellbeing. The raft was all ready bar the oars. A group of the colony's patients came over to give us a farewell serenade that night, with a blind man singing local songs. The band consisted of a flute player, a guitarist and a *bandoneón*[32] player with virtually no fingers, and non-patients helping out with a saxophone, another guitar and some percussion. After that came the speechifying; four patients in turn made us speeches as best they could, a bit clumsily. One of them got stuck and out of desperation shouted, 'Three cheers for the doctors.' Alberto then thanked them for their welcome in glowing terms, saying that the natural beauty of Peru paled in comparison with the emotional beauty of this moment, that he was deeply touched,

[32] A small accordion.

that words failed him except to say, and here he flung open his arms with a Perón-like gesture and intonation, 'A big thank you to all of you.'

The patients cast off and the human cargo drifted away from the shore to the sound of a folk tune, the faint light of the lanterns giving the whole scene a ghostly quality. We went on to Dr Bresciani's house for some drinks, chatted for a while and then to bed.

Friday was departure day so we went to say goodbye to the patients and, after taking some photos, came back bearing two splendid pineapples, a present from Dr Montoya. We bathed and ate, at three o'clock we started saying goodbye and at half past three our raft, named *Mambo-Tango*, set off downriver carrying the crew of us two, and for a while Dr Bresciani and Alfaro, and Chávez who built the raft.

They took us out into the middle of the river and left us there to our own resources.

OUR LITTLE KONTIKI

Two or three mosquitoes weren't enough to beat my longing for sleep and within a few minutes it had won. It was a pyrrhic victory, however, because Alberto's voice shook me from the delicious state of limbo I was in. The faint light of a town, which from the look of it had to be Leticia, appeared on the left bank of the river. We then began the arduous task of getting the raft towards the lights and that's when disaster struck: the contraption categorically refused to move towards the bank, determined to carry on down with the current. We rowed with all our might and just when it looked as if we were on our way, we'd twist right round and were back in midstream again. With growing desperation we watched the lights disappear into the distance. Exhausted, we decided to win the battle with the mosquitoes at least and sleep until dawn when we would figure out what to do. Our situation wasn't very promising. If we carried on downriver we'd have to go as far as Manaus which, according to more or less reliable sources, was about ten days away and, thanks to an accident the day before, we had no fishing hooks left, hardly any provisions, nor were we sure we could get to shore when we wanted to, not to mention the fact that we'd entered Brazil without proper papers and didn't know the language. These worries, however, soon faded as we fell into a deep sleep. I woke with the sun and crawled out of my mosquito net to see what our position was. With the worst will in the world, our little Kontiki had deposited itself on the right bank of the river, and there it was calmly waiting at a kind of little jetty belonging to some nearby house. I decided to leave the inspection for later because the mosquitoes still thought they were within eating range and were having a good bite. Alberto was sleeping like a log so I thought I'd do the same. A morbid languor and a kind of uneasy lethargy had swept over me. I felt incapable of taking a decision but clung to the thought that however bad things got, there was no reason to suppose we couldn't handle it.

LETTER FROM COLOMBIA: BOGOTÁ,
6 JULY 1952

DEAR MUM,
Here I am, a few kilometres further and a few *pesos*
poorer, getting ready to head for Venezuela. First of all, let me
wish you the indispensable happy birthday; I hope you spent it
as happily as ever with the family. Next, I'll be organized, I'll
give you a succinct account of my great adventure since
leaving Iquitos. We set off more or less according to plan; we
travelled for two nights with our faithful retinue of mosquitoes
and arrived in the San Pablo colony at dawn, where we were
given accommodation. The medical director, a marvellous
guy, took to us immediately and, generally speaking, we got on
well with the whole colony, except the nuns who asked why we
didn't go to mass. It turned out these nuns run the place and
anyone who didn't go to mass had their rations cut (we went
without, but the kids helped us and got us something every
day). Apart from this minor cold war, life was incredibly
pleasant. On the 14th, they gave me a party with lots of *pisco*,
a kind of gin which makes you beautifully tipsy. The medical
director toasted us and I, inspired by the booze, replied with a
very Panamerican speech, which earned great applause from
the eminent, and eminently drunk, audience. We stayed a little
longer than planned, but finally set off for Colombia. The
previous night a group of patients came over from the colony
sick zone in a large canoe; they sang us a farewell serenade on
the jetty and made some very touching speeches. Alberto, who
sees himself as Perón's natural heir, delivered such an im-

pressive demagogic speech that our well-wishers were convulsed with laughter. The scene was one of the most interesting of our trip. An accordion player with no fingers on his right hand used little sticks tied to his wrist, the singer was blind and almost all the others were hideously deformed, due to the nervous form of the disease which is very common in this area. With the light from lamps and lanterns reflected in the river, it was like a scene from a horror film. The place is very lovely, completely surrounded by jungle, with aboriginal tribes barely a mile away whom we visited, of course, and an abundance of fish and game to eat everywhere and incalculable potential wealth, all of which set us dreaming of crossing the Mato Grosso by river, from the Paraguay to the Amazon, practising medicine as we go, and so on . . . a dream like having your own home . . . maybe one day . . . We were feeling a bit more like real explorers and set sail downriver on a luxury raft which they built specially for us. The first day went well but at night, instead of keeping watch, we both settled down comfortably to sleep, protected by a mosquito net we'd been given, and woke up to find we'd run aground on the riverbank.

We ate like sharks. The next day passed happily and we decided to keep watch for an hour each to avoid any further problems since at dusk the current had carried us against the bank and some half-submerged branches nearly tipped the raft over. During one of my watches, I earned a black mark when one of the hens we were taking as food fell in the river and the current swept it away. I, who had swum right across the river in San Pablo, hadn't the guts to go in after it, partly because we saw alligators surface now and again and partly because I've never really got over my fear of water at night.

You would have pulled it out if you'd been there, so would Ana María, since you don't have silly night-time complexes like me. One of our hooks caught the most enormous fish and we had our work cut out hauling it aboard. We kept watch until morning, when we tied up to the bank and both crawled under the mosquito net, as there were extra-nasty mosquitoes about. After a good sleep, Alberto, who prefers fish to chicken, discovered our two baited hooks had disappeared during the night, which put him in an even fouler mood and, as there was a house near by, we decided to find out how far it was to Leticia. When the owner told us in proper Portuguese that Leticia was seven hours upriver and that we were now in Brazil, we had a heated argument over which of us had fallen asleep on watch. This got us nowhere. We gave the owner the fish and a pineapple weighing about four kilos which the lepers had given us and stayed overnight in his house before he took us upriver again. The return trip was also very fast, but hard work because we had to row for at least seven hours in a canoe and we weren't used to it. We were well treated in Leticia; they gave us board and lodging, etc., at the police station, but we couldn't get more than 50 per cent off our air fares, and had to fork out 130 Colombian *pesos*, plus another fifteen for excess baggage, making a total of 1,500 Argentine *pesos* in all. What saved the day, though, was that we were asked to coach a football team while we were waiting for the plane which came once a fortnight. Initially we only meant to coach them so they didn't make fools of themselves, but they were so bad we decided to play too, with the brilliant result that what was considered the weakest team went into the one-day championship totally reorganized, got to the final and only lost on penalties. Alberto was inspired by looking a bit like Pedernera[33] with his spot-on passes – he was nicknamed Pedernerita, in fact – and I saved a penalty which will go down in the history of Leticia. The whole celebration would have been great if they hadn't decided to play the Colombian national anthem at the end and I hadn't bent down to wipe some blood off my knee in the middle, which sparked a very violent reaction from the colonel, who shouted at me. I was just about to shout back when I remembered our journey, etc., and bit my tongue. After a great flight in a cocktail-shaker of a plane, we arrived in Bogotá. On the way Alberto chatted to the other passengers and recounted a terrible flight we'd had across the Atlantic once when we had attended an international conference of leprologists in Paris, and how we'd been within an inch of plunging into the Atlantic when three of the four engines failed, ending up with, 'Honestly, these Douglases . . .'; he was so convincing I was even scared myself.

We feel like we've been round the world twice. Our first day in Bogotá went pretty well, we got food on the university campus but no accommodation because it was full of students on grants for courses organized by the UN. No Argentines, of course. Just after one in the morning we were finally put up in the hospital, by which I mean a chair to spend the night in. We aren't all that broke, but explorers of our stature would rather die than pay for the bourgeois comfort of a hostel. After that the leprosy service took us in, even though they had sniffed us with caution the first day because of the letter of introduction we brought from Peru, which was very complimentary but had

---

[33] An Argentine footballer.

been signed Dr Pesce who plays in the same position as Lusteau.[34] Alberto thrust various diplomas under their noses and they hardly had time to catch their breath before I collared them about my work on allergies and left them reeling. The outcome? We were both offered jobs. I had no intention of accepting but Alberto, for obvious reasons, was considering it when, because I'd used Roberto's knife to sketch something on the ground in the street, we had a dust up with the police who harassed us so badly that we decided to leave for Venezuela as soon as possible, so by the time you get this letter, I'll be just about leaving. If you want to chance it, write to Cúcuta, Santander del Norte, Colombia, or very quickly here to Bogotá. Tomorrow I'm going to see Millonarios play Real Madrid in the cheapest stand, since our compatriots are harder to tap than ministers. There is more repression of individual freedom here than in any country we've been to, the police patrol the streets carrying rifles and demand your papers every few minutes, which some of them read upside down. The atmosphere is tense and a revolution may be brewing. The countryside is in open revolt and the army is powerless to put it down. The Conservatives fight among themselves and can't agree, and the memory of 9 April 1948[35] still weighs heavily on everyone's minds. In short, it's suffocating here. If the Colombians want to put up with it, good luck to them, but we're getting out of here as soon as we can. Alberto has a good chance of a job in Caracas apparently.

[34] An Argentine footballer who played on the left wing.
[35] When the radical Liberal politician Jorge Eliécer Gaitán was murdered.

I hope someone will scribble a few lines to let me know how you are. You won't have to glean information through Beatriz this time (I'm not replying to her because we're limiting ourselves to one letter per city, which is why the card for Alfredito Gabela is enclosed).

Love from your son, who misses you from head to toe. Let's hope the old man gets himself up to Venezuela, the cost of living is higher than here, but the pay is much better and that should suit a skinflint (!) like him. By the way, if he's still in love with Uncle Sam after living up here for a while ... but don't let's get sidetracked, Dad can read between the lines. Ciao.

TO CARACAS

A FTER the usual unnecessary questions, the pawing and messing about with passports and the inquisitorial looks typical of suspicious policemen, they gave us a vast official stamp with a departure date of 14 July, and we began walking across the bridge which unites and separates the two countries. A Venezuelan soldier, with the same peevish insolence as his Colombian counterparts – apparently a trait common to all military stock – checked our baggage and then submitted us to his own personal interrogation just to show who was boss. They kept us quite a while in San Antonio de Táchira for purely administrative formalities, and then we carried on in the minibus which had promised to take us to San Cristóbal. Halfway there is the customs post where we underwent a thorough search of our baggage and persons. The famous knife which had caused so much hassle in Bogotá again proved the excuse for a long discussion which we conducted with masterly experience of arguments with such highly cultured persons as police sergeants. The revolver got through because it was in the pocket of my leather jacket, in a grime-caked bundle which scared off the customs guys. The knife, which had been re-covered with such difficulty, was a new worry because there were customs posts all the way to Caracas and we weren't sure of always finding brains which could cope with the elementary reasons we gave them. The road linking the two frontier towns is perfectly paved, especially the Venezuelan side, and reminds me a lot of the hills around Córdoba. It would seem that this country is generally more prosperous than Colombia.

When we reached San Cristóbal, an argument ensued between the owners of the transport company and ourselves who wanted to travel in the cheapest possible way. For the first time on our trip, the thesis propounding the advantages of travelling for two days by minibus, rather than three in a bus, won the day. Anxious to get on with future plans and treat my asthma properly, we decided to part with an extra twenty *bolívares*,[36] sacrificing them in honour of Caracas. We filled in time until evening, walking around and reading something about the country in quite a good library they have there.

At eleven o'clock we set off northward, leaving all trace of asphalt behind. In a seat already too small for three people, they squashed four of us, so there was not a hope in hell of sleeping. Besides, a flat tyre set us back an hour and my asthma

[36] Venezuelan currency.

146

was still bothering me. When we climbed slowly to the summit, the vegetation was scarcer, but in the valleys the same kinds of crops as in Colombia were growing. The badly maintained roads cause loads of punctures and we had several on our second day. The police have control points which check all minibuses thoroughly and we'd have been in a mess if it hadn't been for the letter of recommendation one woman passenger had; the driver said all the luggage was hers, end of story. Meals had become more expensive and one *bolívar* per head had risen to three and a half. We decided to spend as little as possible, so we didn't eat at the Punta del Águila stop, but the driver took pity on our plight and bought us a good meal. Punta del Águila is the highest part of the Venezuelan Andes, rising to 4,108 metres above sea level. I took my last two tablets so I slept pretty well. In the morning, the driver stopped for an hour to sleep because he'd been driving for two days non-stop. We expected to arrive in Caracas that night but were delayed by flat tyres again and the wiring was faulty as well so the battery wouldn't charge and we had to stop to fix it. The climate had turned tropical with fierce mosquitoes and bananas everywhere. The last stretch of road which I did while semi-dozing, with a bad attack of asthma, was perfectly asphalted and seemed to be very pretty (it was dark by then). Dawn was just breaking as we arrived at our destination. I was absolutely knackered. I flopped down on a bed we rented for 0.50 *bolívares* and slept the sleep of the dead, with the help of an adrenalin injection Alberto gave me.

THIS STRANGE TWENTIETH CENTURY

T HE WORST of my asthma attack is over and I feel almost all right, though now and again I resort to my new acquisition, a French inhaler. It's extraordinary how much I miss Alberto. It's as if my flanks are unprotected from a hypothetical attack. I'm always turning round to tell him something and then I realize he's not there.

Well, there's not much to complain about: painstakingly well looked after, good food in abundance and the expectation of going home to start my studies again and finally getting the degree which will enable me to practise. Yet the idea of saying goodbye definitively doesn't make me altogether happy; all those months we've been together through thick and thin and the habit of dreaming the same dreams in similar situations has made us even closer.

Turning all these ideas over in my head, I drift away from the centre of Caracas and walk towards the suburbs, where the houses are much wider apart. Caracas extends along a narrow valley which encloses it and limits it sideways, so that you can't go very far without having to climb the surrounding hills and there, with the dynamic city spread at your feet, you see a new feature of its heterogeneous make-up. The blacks, those magnificent examples of the African race who have conserved their racial purity by a lack of affinity with washing, have seen their patch invaded by a different kind of slave: the Portuguese. And the two ancient races now share a common experience, fraught with bickering and squabbling. Discrimination and poverty unite them in a daily battle for survival but their different attitudes to life separate them completely: the black is indolent and fanciful, he spends his money on frivolity and drink; the European comes from a tradition of working and saving which follows him to this corner of America and drives him to get ahead, even independently of his own individual aspirations.

This far up the hill concrete houses have totally given way to adobe huts. I peep into one. It is a room half separated by a partition with a fire and table on one side and on the other piles of straw which seem to serve as beds. Several bony cats and a mangy dog are playing with three naked black kids. Acrid smoke from the fire fills the room. The black mother, with frizzy hair and droopy breasts, is preparing the food, helped by a girl of about fifteen, who is fully dressed. We start chatting and after a while I ask if I can take a photo of them which they categorically refuse to accept unless I give it to them straight away. I try to explain that I have to develop it first, but no, they want it straight away or nothing doing. I eventually say yes, but now they're suspicious and won't co-operate. One of the kids scampers off to play with his friends while I carry on talking to the family. In the end, I stand at the door with my camera ready and pretend to snap anyone who sticks their head out. We fool around like this for a while until I see the little kid come nonchalantly back on a new bicycle; I get him in focus and press the button but the effect is disastrous. To avoid the photo, the kid swerves, falls off and bursts into tears. They all instantly stop being camera-shy and come rushing out hurling abuse at me. I withdraw with some trepidation because they are great stone throwers, followed by the family's insults, amongst which is, the height of contempt: 'Portuguese.'

Dotted along the sides of the road are crates for transporting cars which the Portuguese use to live in. In one of these, with a black family in it, I glimpse a brand new fridge, and blaring out of many of them is music from radios with the volume turned full up. Shiny new cars are parked outside the most miserable dwellings. Planes of all types fly overhead sowing the sky with noise and silvery glints while at my feet lies Caracas, the city of eternal spring. Its historic centre is threatened by the encroaching red of tiled roofs mixed with the flat roofs of modern constructions. But there is something which will make the yellowy tones of its colonial buildings live on even after they have disappeared: the spirit of Caracas, impervious to the way of life of the North and stubbornly rooted in its retrograde semi-pastoral colonial past.

AS AN AFTERTHOUGHT[37]

THE STARS streaked the night sky with light in that little mountain town, and the silence and the cold dematerialized the darkness. It was – I don't really know how to explain it – as if all solid substances were spirited away in the ethereal space around us, denying our individuality and submerging us, rigid, in the immense blackness. There was not a single cloud to give the space perspective by blocking a portion of the starry sky. Only at a few metres from me did the dim light of a lamp fade the darkness around it.

The man's face was lost in the shadow; all I could see were the two sparks of his eyes and the white of his four front teeth.

[37] Apparently written after Ernesto got home, it is not clear in which country and when this episode took place.

I still don't know whether it was the atmosphere or the man's personality which prepared me for the revelation, but I'd heard those same arguments many times from different people and they had made no impression on me. The speaker was, in fact, a very interesting man. Fleeing the knife of dogmatism in a European country as a young man, he had tasted fear (one of the few experiences that make you value life) and then, wandering from country to country, clocking up thousands of adventures, he had ended up in this isolated region waiting patiently for the great moment to arrive.

After the introductory trivialities and niceties, when the conversation was faltering and we were about to go our separate ways, he let slip, with that cheeky laugh of his, accentuating the disparity of his four front incisors: 'The future belongs to the people and gradually or suddenly they will take power, here and all over the world.

'The problem is,' he went on, 'that the people need to be educated and they can't do that before taking power, only after. They can only learn by their own mistakes, and these will be very serious and will cost many innocent lives. Or maybe not, maybe those lives are not innocent because they'll belong to those who commit the huge sin *contra natura*; in other words, they lack the ability to adapt. All of them, all those who can't adapt – you and I, for instance – will die cursing the power which they helped bring about with often enormous sacrifices. Revolution is impersonal, so it will take their lives and even use their memory as an example or as an instrument to control the young people coming after them. My sin is greater because I, more subtle or more experienced, call it what you like, will die knowing that my sacrifice stems only from a stubbornness which symbolizes our rotten crumbling civilization. I also know – and this won't change the course of history or your personal impression of me – that you will die with your fist clenched and your jaw tense, the perfect manifestation of hatred and struggle, because you aren't a symbol (some inanimate example), you are an authentic member of the society to be destroyed; the spirit of the beehive speaks through your mouth and moves through your actions. You are as useful as I am, but you don't realize how useful your contribution is to the society that sacrifices you.'

I saw his teeth and the playful grin with which he foretold history, I felt his handshake and, like a distant murmur, his conventional goodbye. The night, which folded away as his words touched it, closed in around me again, enveloping me within it. Despite what he said, I now knew ... I knew that when the great guiding spirit cleaves humanity into two antagonistic halves, I will be with the people. And I know it because I see it imprinted on the night that I, the eclectic dissector of doctrines and psychoanalyst of dogmas, howling like a man possessed, will assail the barricades and trenches, will stain my weapon with blood and, consumed with rage, will slaughter any enemy I lay hands on. And then, as if an immense weariness were consuming my recent exhilaration, I see myself being sacrificed to the authentic revolution, the great leveller of individual will, pronouncing the exemplary *mea culpa*. I feel my nostrils dilate, savouring the acrid smell of gunpowder and blood, of the enemy's death; I brace my body, ready for combat, and prepare myself to be a sacred precinct within which the bestial howl of the victorious proletariat can resound with new vigour and new hope.

Epilogue: Ernesto Goes to Miami and Back to Buenos Aires

BY ERNESTO GUEVARA LYNCH

W HILE Granado stayed in Venezuela, Ernesto went on to Miami in a plane transporting racehorses. The plane was scheduled to be there only a day, then return to Caracas and back to Argentina, but the captain decided to have the engines given a thorough check in Miami and one was found to have a serious fault. The engine had to be repaired. It took a whole month to sort out and Ernesto, who had to fly back on the same plane, was stranded in Miami with just one dollar in his pocket. He was hard pushed to survive thirty days on that slender capital. He stayed in a small hotel promising to pay from Buenos Aires, which he did.

When he got home, he told us about the hard time he'd had without any money. An exaggerated sense of pride had prevented him from letting us know. Nearly every day he walked from his hotel in the city centre out to the holiday beaches, because only rarely did he manage to get a lift; if I remember rightly, it was about fifteen kilometres. But he enjoyed himself as much as he could and got to know the United States, at least a small part of it.

When the plane was repaired, he boarded it for the return journey. Flying into Caracas, a stable boy who had also been stranded in Miami woke him to tell him that the undercarriage had jammed and they were circling the Venezuelan capital. The plane was carrying a large cargo of crates of fruit, but they were the only passengers. Ernesto thought he was joking and went back to sleep, only to wake a little later and look out of the window to see a huge array of lorries, cars and fire engines. The undercarriage really had jammed and the captain had advised the control tower to alert staff for an emergency landing. Fortunately, they succeeded in unjamming the wheel mechanism and touched down without mishap shortly afterwards.

One morning in Buenos Aires we received a message that Ernesto was arriving that afternoon in a cargo plane from Miami. He was finally coming home after a journey which had lasted eight months and taken him through a good part of South America.

Our whole family went to Ezeiza airport to meet him. The sky that afternoon was overcast, the low clouds hindering visibility. Few aircraft were flying. The cargo plane had been due to arrive at two o'clock and we'd already been waiting for two hours. We were all very nervous because there was no sight of the plane and it had not been in contact with the control tower either. They calmed us down by telling us cargo planes didn't have fixed schedules and usually turned up on the runway when they were least expected.

And so it was. The Douglas suddenly appeared, flying low through the clouds, and circling wide over the airport it landed with no trouble at all. A few moments later, a raincoat sheltering him from the drizzle, Ernesto came out and ran towards the terminal. I was on the terrace and, cupping my hands like a megaphone, shouted for all I was worth. He heard the shout but couldn't see where it came from. Then he spotted us on the terrace and I still remember his smiling face as he waved to us. It was September 1952.

CRITICAL STUDIES IN
LATIN AMERICAN AND IBERIAN CULTURE

SERIES EDITORS:

James Dunkerley
John King

This major series – the first of its kind to appear in English – is designed to map the field of contemporary Latin American culture, which has enjoyed increasing popularity in Britain and the United States in recent years.

The series aims to broaden the scope of criticism of Latin American culture, which tends still to extol the virtues of a few established 'master' works, and to examine cultural production within the context of twentieth-century history. These clear, accessible studies are aimed at those who wish to know more about some of the most important and influential cultural works and movements of our time.

Other Titles in the Series

156